# CREATED BY GOD

## ABOUT HUMAN SEXUALITY FOR OLDER GIRLS AND BOYS

(Plus the Loving Adults Who Watch and Help Them Grow)

W9-BYG-958

# Created by God: About Human Sexuality for Older Girls and Boys
## (Plus the Loving Adults Who Watch and Help Them Grow)

ISBN 13: 978-0-687-07409-9

For permission to reproduce any material in this publication, write to
Permissions Office, 201 Eighth Avenue, South, P.O. Box 801, Nashville, TN 37202-0801.
You may FAX your request to 615-749-6128.

Scripture quotations in this publication, unless otherwise identified, are from the *New Revised Standard Version* of the Bible, copyrighted © 1989 by the Division of Christian Education of the National Council of the Churches of Christ in the United States of America, and are used by permission. All rights reserved.

James H. Ritchie, Jr., Editor
Betsi H. Smith, Production Editor
R.E. Osborne, Production and Design Manager
Paige Easter, Designer
Ron Benedict, Cover Photo
John Beale, Back Cover Photo

**Art Credits:**
Pages 4, 8, 11, 13, 15, 16, 18, 20, 22, 24, 26, 27, 41, 58, 61, 62, 64, 66, 71,
72, 73, 75, 78, 80, 93, 96, 98, 100, 102, 110, 112, 114, 123, 128, 135, and 137:
Robbie Short; © 1999 Abingdon Press.
Pages 29, 32, 35, 37, 45, 51, 52, 53, 87, 89, and 91: Sarah Smith,
Linden Artists, Ltd.; © 1999 Abingdon Press.

08 09 10–18 17 16 15 14 13
MANUFACTURED IN THE UNITED STATES OF AMERICA

**Acknowledgment**
The contributions of Dorlis Brown Glass to *God Made Us: About Sex and Growing Up* in 1980 and to *Created by God: About Human Sexuality for Older Girls and Boys* in 1989 are acknowledged with great appreciation. Her love, experience, and expertise continue to leave a significant imprint on this resource, fashioned for young persons and parents of the new millennium.

# CREATED BY GOD

## ABOUT HUMAN SEXUALITY
## FOR OLDER GIRLS AND BOYS

(Plus the Loving
Adults Who Watch and
Help Them Grow)

Revised and updated by James H. Ritchie, Jr., Ed.D.

# CONTENTS

Introduction      6

Chapter 1      8
Change!

Chapter 2      23
A Marvelous Creation Tale:
What Makes Us Female, What Makes Us Male

Chapter 3      39
Inside and Out: How Change Comes About

Chapter 4      63
Being Female, Being Male, Being You

Chapter 5      79
A New Life Begins

Chapter 6      101
Look Inside the Question Box

Glossary      138

# INTRODUCTION

## You, my friend, are being created by God! Sound odd?

**T**he fact that you were created by God sounds familiar. God created everything, and you certainly qualify as part of everything. But *being* created? What's *that* all about?

It's about this: You are a work in progress, and I guarantee that over the next few years, you are going to make some mind-boggling progress! The person you are in the process of becoming may soon look almost unrecognizable when compared to the person you are right now.

That's because God is still at work in you, creating the person God had in mind from the very beginning. The beginning of what? How about the beginning of everything! In talking with God about all of this, the writer of Psalm 139 said:

For it was you who formed my inward parts;
you knit me together in my mother's womb.
I praise you, for I am fearfully
and wonderfully made.
Wonderful are your works;
that I know very well.
My frame was not hidden from you,
when I was being made in secret,
intricately woven in the depths of the earth.
Your eyes beheld my unformed substance.
In your book were written all the days
that were formed for me,
when none of them as yet existed.
Psalm 139:13-16

In short, God has had you in mind from the very beginning. God has also had in mind a path by which you would move from childhood to adulthood. You've been walking that path since you were born, but now it's time for your leisurely stroll to shift into a jog (maybe even a full-blown run?). These next few years will find you making major steps toward being an adult—major steps in how you look, how you feel, how you think, and how you connect with other persons.

God's incredible act of creation continues! Along with parents and the other folks who love you, watch you grow, and walk beside you in the process, I hope you will better understand and celebrate the special person you are and the special person you are becoming.

You, my friend, are being wonderfully created by God. And, by the way, God is doing an excellent job!

James H. Ritchie, Jr., Ed.D.

7

# CHAPTER

## Change!

A Snapshot of God's Son
Son of the Law
It's Called "Adolescence"
You Too!
Growing in Wisdom
Deep Breaths!
Families Change as You Change
Belonging to God's Family

# A Snapshot of God's Son

The Bible offers only one glimpse of Jesus between his birth and his baptism 30 years later. That's all we have. The good news is that this "snapshot" captures an image of Jesus when he was about your age. Like you, Jesus was growing and changing.

Have you ever wondered how Jesus felt about growing up? what he liked to do? what he worried about? who his friends were? what they did together? if he was ever afraid? if he got bored with chores he was expected to do or lessons he was expected to learn? Do you think he ever spent time daydreaming as you do? What do you think he looked forward to when he thought about what it would be like to be "all grown up"? What were the signals that helped him know he was maturing as a person and as God's child?

# Son of the Law

You can find this story in your Bible by turning to Luke 2:41-52.

Imagine this scene. Daylight has not yet dawned on the town of Nazareth, but the last minutes of darkness are full of anything but quiet. If you have ever gotten up very early to leave on a trip, you know what this might have been like.

"Hurry, Son!" Joseph calls from the doorway of his carpenter's shop. "The caravan will be leaving for Jerusalem very soon. I need your help loading supplies on the donkeys."

A short time later the pilgrimage begins. The Passover journey was one Jesus and his parents had been making for years.

Together with other Jewish pilgrims they traveled south toward Jerusalem every spring. There they worshiped in the Temple and joined with friends and family in a meal that used special words, foods, and actions to remind them how God had delivered the people of Israel from Egyptian slavery many years before.

But this time the Passover would be different. Mary and Joseph had been thinking about, talking about, and planning for this trip since the day Jesus was born. Although at twelve he still had lots of growing to do, Jesus was, according to Jewish tradition, officially becoming an adult—a bar mitzvah—"son of command" or "son of the Law." Jesus would begin to have new responsibilities for helping to keep the faith alive. He would have new privileges, such as worshiping with the men. He also would be expected to make wise choices. In many ways this visit to Jerusalem and to the Temple would celebrate his growing up.

Imagine that, like all such caravans in Bible times, this one is accompanied by the jingle of camel bells, the bray of donkeys, and the laughter of children. The days of travel go by quickly. Soon the company of pilgrims makes its way along the narrow, twisting road from Jericho to Jerusalem. Picture them the night before their arrival in

JERUSALEM

Jerusalem, camping near an inn. While the adults exchange news and stories around the campfires, the children chatter on about the beautiful Temple and the marvelous city they would soon be visiting.

Jesus might have announced to his friends, "I was born just a few miles from Jerusalem—in Bethlehem. When I was eight days old, my parents took me to the Temple and dedicated me to God." The others join in with stories that had been told about their dedications and share memories of earlier trips to Jerusalem. They tell of their plans for this Passover adventure.

At first light they break camp and start out on the last leg of their journey. Rounding a bend in the road, Jesus looks up at the massive walls and great watchtowers of Jerusalem that overlook the roads and valleys below. His heart pounds with anticipation. He and Joseph had talked many times about this trip. The pictures in his mind are clear. He knows that the experience will be an unforgettable one. Eagerly Jesus and his friends run ahead, reaching the city gate before the others. Dancing impatiently, they await the arrival of the rest of the caravan.

For the next several days Jesus explores the city. Every day he visits the Temple and watches the sacrifices being offered to God—one of the privileges of being considered an adult. A full participant now in the Temple worship, he listens eagerly as the teachers read and explain the meaning of God's Law. Although he had often heard many of the words before, he understands them this time in new and exciting ways.

The days in Jerusalem are full, and all too soon the Passover comes to a close. On the day they are to return to Nazareth, the women and children, generally moving more slowly, depart earlier than the men. As Mary makes one last check to be sure that everything had been packed on the donkeys, she might be wondering why Jesus isn't there to help. With a smile she remembers; and as the caravan begins to move, she sighs and says to herself, "How quickly things change! Last year Jesus was here at my side. Now he is a bar mitzvah and travels with his father and the rest of the men. I'm sure that my grownup son will have lots of stories to tell at the fire this evening!"

As Joseph and the other men prepare to leave the city, he assumes that Jesus is traveling with his mother, just as he had always done. "My son," he chuckles to himself, "an adult!" Joseph knows the tradition of his people, but he also knows that Jesus is at that awkward age—no longer a child and not yet an adult.

Evening comes, and the men catch up with the women. Together they begin to prepare the campsite. Mary and Joseph realize for the first time that Jesus is not with either of them. Anxiously they move through the caravan, stopping at the tents and cooking fires of friends and family to ask if anyone has seen Jesus. Convinced that Jesus is not with the company of Passover pilgrims, they hurriedly collect their belongings and head back a day's journey toward Jerusalem.

13

For three days they search the city. Jesus has now been missing for five days. On their fourth day back in the city, they make their way to the Temple that had so fascinated Jesus during this Passover trip. There he is, sitting at the feet of the teachers, listening carefully to all they had to say. There was so much to absorb—how would he ever take it all in? The teachers are amazed by the understanding reflected in the questions Jesus asks.

Feelings of relief flood over Joseph and Mary as they realize that Jesus is safe—feelings that quickly turn to bewilderment and even a bit of anger. Why would Jesus do such a thing? Jesus sees the worry on his parents' faces and hears the fear in their voices. "Didn't you know that I had to be in my Father's house?" Jesus asks, sounding surprised that his parents didn't know where he would be.

But they hadn't known, and they didn't understand all the changes that were taking place in their son. They also didn't understand how the changes Jesus was experiencing were causing changes in the family. And this was not the last time that they would be puzzled by Jesus' behavior. For now, Mary would tuck this incident away in her mind, where she could take it out from time to time and try once again to grasp what had happened. Someday, perhaps, she would understand.

Joseph, Mary, and Jesus make the journey back to Nazareth together. There are times when they talk and times when they are silent—unable to find words to express their feelings about all that was happening. The story ends with these words: "And Jesus increased in wisdom and in years [getting wiser and older], and in divine and human favor [gaining the approval of God and other persons]" (Luke 2:52).

# It's Called "Adolescence"

**A**s Jesus traveled with his family to Jerusalem and back, he was also traveling through *adolescence (a-doh-LES-sens)—the period of growth between childhood and adulthood. Like you, he was growing, wondering, testing, and discovering. While his family remained important to him, he also was developing relationships outside his family.

Where once he might have contented himself to play on the floor of his father's carpenter shop, drawing pictures in the sawdust and building towers from scraps of wood, Jesus now worked and learned at his father's side—lifting, measuring, sawing, hammering, and carving. He no longer had the body of a child. New muscles and new coordination helped Jesus take on new responsibilities.

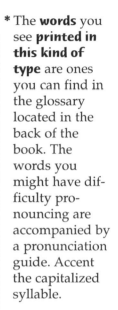

* The **words** you see **printed in this kind of type** are ones you can find in the glossary located in the back of the book. The words you might have difficulty pronouncing are accompanied by a pronunciation guide. Accent the capitalized syllable.

# You Too!

**T**hink about how you have grown and changed in the past few years. That baldheaded little person pictured in the family photo album was you not so long ago. On the following page of the album might be a picture of a crying toddler showing Grandpa a skinned elbow or knee. Then there's the one of your first day of school, of your first dance recital, of you in your soccer or Scout uniform, or of you in the children's program at church. How you've grown! Wasn't it just the other day that someone mentioned how many jeans sizes you've gone through this past year?

Have you wondered, *Am I supposed to be growing this fast? Should I be growing faster? How long is this going to continue? Why can't I look like everybody else? Do other kids feel as awkward as I do? Am I weird?*

Your body is changing in ways other than size. In fact, it could very well be that you haven't noticed much difference in your height or weight as of yet. That's perfectly OK. But change is happening. Many of the changes are going on inside your body, where neither you nor anyone else can see them.

You may be noticing changes in your energy level. One moment you've got energy to spare, and the next you're so tired, you could drop. Then there are changes in mood or emotions. You suddenly shift without warning from laughing happily with longtime friends to shouting at them as though they were longtime enemies. Confused parents just shake their heads. If only they knew the confusion you feel at times!

Do you suppose that Jesus felt this way too?

# Growing in Wisdom

**J**esus was growing wiser. You might wonder, *Does that mean he didn't know everything from the very beginning?* No, he didn't. He grew up just as you are doing—just as all of us do. As his body matured, so did his mind. He grew in his ability to make choices based on what he knew and on how his decisions would affect others. He was learning to live responsibly.

You're trying to live responsibly too. You're becoming aware that what you do affects many persons, not just yourself. You're more aware of the needs of persons who don't have homes; of families who don't have adequate food or medical care; of persons whose lives have been turned upside down by a flood, a fire, or a tornado. You get angry when you see people treated unfairly. You may be wondering what you can do to help. You ask questions and look for solutions. You sometimes feel frustrated because adults don't always take you seriously.

At times you find yourself questioning things you've always believed to be true, including things about God. You wonder, *Is it all right to doubt?* You feel impatient when others expect you to think as they do or expect you to think as you have always thought in the past.

Sometimes you're impatient with people who keep telling you to grow up when you're not convinced that you're ready to turn loose of the child you have been all your life. You may discover that changes in the way you look at situations, and your questioning of the way things have always been, cause people to get upset. Jesus certainly discovered that changes taking place in him were disrupting the lives of his parents!

Deep down, you know what Jesus knew as he sat with the teachers in the Temple. Asking questions is important. You are learning to set goals for yourself. You are preparing for the future. You need information and understanding if you are to grow in wisdom as Jesus did.

# Deep Breaths!

The way you feel about others may be changing too. You want to share your dreams with the people who are important to you. Then again, you want privacy—quiet times in which to explore your dreams. You want to be more independent, to make your own decisions and to take greater control of your life; but not everyone is ready to allow you that independence. The truth is, even *you* may question how ready you are to become more independent.

Confused? Who wouldn't be! Life for a young person traveling into and through adolescence can be much like a wild roller coaster ride complete with all the steep climbs, sudden plunges, twists, turns, and corkscrews. When they take the time to think back, most adults—including parents—remember the feelings connected with their own roller coaster rides through adolescence.

Growing up can't be rushed. It takes time for bodies to grow and develop. It takes time for us to learn through study and experience to make responsible decisions. It takes time for us to learn how to live with others in Christlike love and respect.

Though you don't remember it, for several months you waited in your mother's **womb** (WOOM) to be born. Now you find yourself waiting once again—waiting to get started with, to get on with, or to get finished with a period of growth as dramatic as that spent in the warm quietness of the womb. A word of advice: Take regular deep breaths, try to relax, and hang on to your sense of humor. As you wait, wonder, breathe, and laugh, think about how the Bible uses the same word for "spirit" that it does for "breath." God's Spirit, like the air we breathe, gives us life and the ability to pace ourselves as we run the course of adolescence.

# Families Change as You Change

You don't run alone. Though they sometimes have trouble keeping up, families run along at our side as we grow and change. "Family" means different things to different people because families are just as unique as individual persons are. When asked, "What is a family?" young persons answer:

A family is a group of people who are related to one another.
A family cares about one another.
A family helps one another.
A family laughs with you when you're happy and cries with you when you're sad.
A family usually lives together—then again, they don't always.

Some families have two parents, some have one, some have three or more. Some families have one child, others have more. Couples without children still consider themselves to be a family. Some families are "blended families," with children born to one of the parents but not to both. Some are "birth" families; others are adopted families. Some families have grandparents, cousins, aunts, and uncles living together. Some families are foster families—families that care for children who are not related to that family by birth or by legal adoption. Regardless of how well our families fit the traditional idea of what it takes to be a family, they are still families.

Your family, no matter what it looks like, experienced a major change when you arrived on the scene. When you were a baby, people cared for all of your needs. As you have grown older, you have been more and more capable of taking care of yourself. Now you are in the process of learning to care for others. As you have grown and changed, so has your family. That's an important idea for you to think about. Families aren't names; they aren't addresses; they aren't houses. Families are persons. As persons change, the families they are

a part of change as well. You sometimes wish that everything else in your life would stay exactly the same while you are going through this time of change. After all, enough is enough!

The wish is understandable, but it won't happen. And you really wouldn't want it to. Change means that parents begin to trust you to do things that you weren't allowed to do when you were younger: spending the day shopping downtown or at a mall with a friend; doing some babysitting for neighbors; or finding other ways to earn personal spending money.

Change also means new limitations. Some of the actions that were acceptable from you as a child are no longer appropriate. Now that you are moving toward adulthood, you can say with the apostle Paul, "I put an end to childish ways" (1 Corinthians 13:11). Families are an important part of discovering what is appropriate and what isn't. As you and your family grow and change together, you will be making such discoveries.

# Belonging to God's Family

**A**ll of us have one thing in common. We were each created in the image of God. You've heard people say something like, "Jessie is the spitting image of her mother!" They are saying that either in her appearance or in her actions, Jessie is much like her mother. You and I were created by God. We were created in the image of God—created like God (Genesis 1:26-27). What is there about us that identifies us as belonging to God's family and therefore being like God?

Like God, you have a hand in the creation of something new—the new person you are becoming. Many of the

21

changes you are experiencing and will experience are factors over which you have no control. Others will call for decisions on your part. Most of these decisions involve your relationships with other people. Those relationships are important things that you take part in creating. The decisions you make will, in part, help to shape the person you will become. You, God, your family, and the other significant people in your life share that important task.

"And Jesus increased in wisdom and in years, and in divine and human favor." The same thing is happening to you. Change is taking place inside you and all around you. Welcome to adolescence, my friend! You are a growing, changing child of God!

# CHAPTER 2

# A Marvelous Creation Tale: What Makes Us Female, What Makes Us Male

In the Beginning

Becoming Adult

The Fantastic Female

The Marvelous Male

The Inside Story: Females

The Inside Story: Males

**23**

# In the Beginning

"**O**h, I already know all that stuff!" said Brenda to a friend when she heard that her church was planning a study on human sexuality. "Me, too!" said the friend.

Maybe you're saying the same thing. After all, you and your friends talk some (and maybe giggle some) about sex. You discuss it every once in a while with a parent or another adult. You have an older brother or sister who answers your questions from time to time. You've read a book on the subject, or you've seen THE FILM about sex that is shown at school once you reach a certain grade.

So, let's agree that you already know some important stuff about how your body functions. Most girls know about what's happening to girls' bodies, and most boys know about what's happening to boys' bodies. However, most girls are curious and could use some additional information about boys. Likewise, most boys are curious and could use some additional information about girls. So, here's a chance to see the whole picture!

In the beginning when God created the heavens and the earth
. . . God said, "Let us make humankind in our image, according
to our likeness" . . . So God created humankind in the image
of God . . . male and female God created them. God blessed them,
and God said to them, "Be fruitful and multiply, and fill the earth
and subdue it; and have dominion over the fish
of the sea and over the birds of the air and over every living
thing that moves upon the earth . . ." God saw everything
that had been made, and indeed, it was very good.

Genesis 1:1, 26-28, and 31, adapted

Our story of human growth and development begins with
God. The Creation story we read in the first two chapters of
Genesis tells about the beginning of life. The most important
information contained there tells us who was responsible,
answering the question, *Who did it?*

God was responsible. We are part of God's creation and a
valuable part of God's plan. What does it mean to be made
like God? It means that we have within us the ability to create—to create beauty, to create peace, to create loving relationships, and even to create new life. For the creation of new life
God made us male and female. This kind of creating calls for
the cooperation of people who are different from each other
in many important ways. The fact that God created two different genders of human beings reminds us of the interdepen-
dence of humankind. We need each other in order to become
all that God has planned for us.

**25**

# Becoming Adult

Changes are taking place in your body right now—some of them seen, but most of them unseen. These changes are preparing you to realize fully the joy that God has planned for people to experience with their bodies. Think about how good it feels to stretch when you get out of bed in the morning. Thank God for that good body-feeling! As you grow, you become more coordinated. Your body is able to move in ways that help you with such things as athletics, dancing, and walking without tripping over your own feet! The cooperation of body parts that comes with growing up is another gift of God.

As you grow and develop, you are becoming aware of how good it feels when someone you care about gives you a hug to say, "I love you," touches you gently when you're upset, or pats you on the back when you've done something well. Becoming an adult means focusing more on others and on their needs than on yourself. Becoming an adult means getting better at caring for people through kind touches and kind words.

Finally, the changes that are going on inside and out indicate that your body is being prepared for the possibility of parenthood.

Changes are easier to deal with when we have some idea of what to expect and are able to talk about them. In order to talk, we need to make sure we are working with a common vocabulary related to the parts of our bodies that make us male and female, and how these body parts function. So, let's begin our tour of female and male bodies.

# The Fantastic Female

**W**e start with the parts we can see. The word **genitals** (JEN-uh-tuhls), or **genitalia** (JEN-uh-TAIL-yuh), refers to the external (on the outside of the body) sex organs of both females and males, sometimes called the "privates." **Vulva** (VUL-vuh) is the name for the female genitals, located below the **abdomen** (AB-doh-men) or belly and between the legs. It's helpful for girls to use a hand-held mirror in order to better see and understand this part of their bodies.

The vulva has several separate structures. At the center is the opening to the **urethra** (yoo-REE-thruh), which is the narrow tube that allows urine to pass from the bladder outside the body. Below the urethral opening is the opening to the **vagina** (vuh-JIE-nuh), the passageway that leads to the internal reproductive organs.

Surrounding the opening to the vagina are two thick folds of skin called the outer or major **labia** (LAY-bee-uh). The word *labia* means "lips," which is sometimes what these folds of skin are called. A second set of folds of skin, the inner or minor labia, are inside and sometimes hidden by the outer labia. The **clitoris** (KLIT-uh-ris) is a small cylinder-shaped organ located where the labia meet at the top of the vulva. The most sensitive part of the vulva, the clitoris, in grown women is about the size of the eraser on a pencil, and is made up of the **shaft** and the **glans** (glanz) or tip. It is covered by another fold of skin, the **clitoral** (KLIT-uh-rul) **hood**. This hood may need to be gently pulled back in order to see the tip of the clitoris and in order to cleanse the genital area when bathing.

# Female Reproductive System
## (external view)

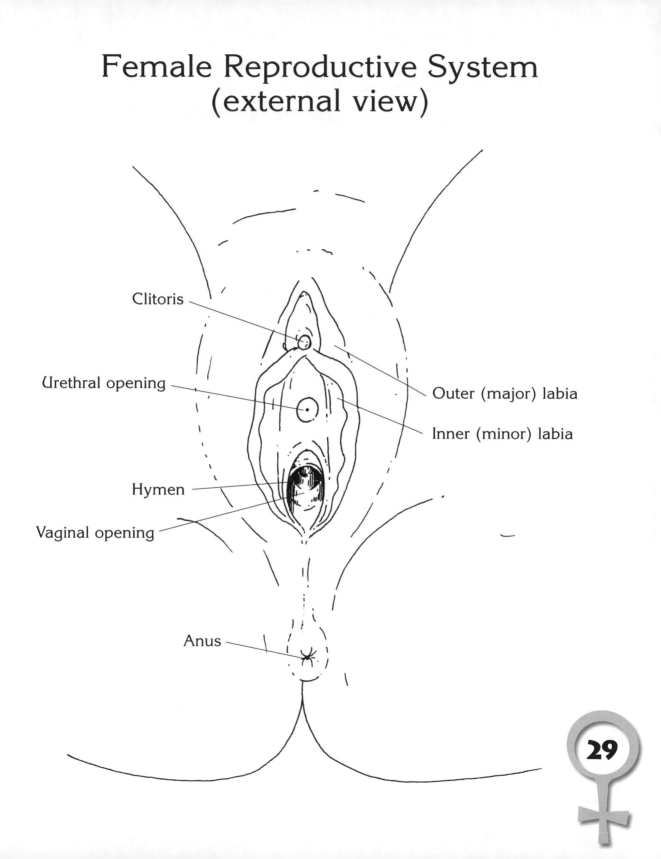

Clitoris

Urethral opening

Outer (major) labia

Inner (minor) labia

Hymen

Vaginal opening

Anus

29

Just inside the opening to the vagina is a thin layer of tissue called the **hymen** (HI-muhn). Extending across the vagina, the hymen contains one or more perforations or openings. It may be torn during vigorous athletic activity or stretching movement or during the first experience of sexual intercourse. Some women are born without a hymen. Because there can be a small amount of bleeding when the hymen is first torn, that blood was once believed to be evidence that a woman had never had sexual intercourse. We now know that this is not the case.

Just above all these structures is a mound of flesh that sticks out a little bit called the **mons** (mahnz). Underneath is a pad of fat tissue that covers and protects the pubic bone. The **anus** (AY-nuhs), the opening where solid waste leaves the body, is not part of the vulva, but is located in the same general area, just below the vulva.

# The Marvelous Male

**R**emember that the external sex organs of males, as with females, are called the genitals. The male genitals have two main parts. The first is the **penis** (PEE-nuhs), the cylinder-shaped organ that gets called everything but a penis. The cylinder part of the penis is called the **shaft**. The end or head of the penis is called the glans and, like the clitoris in the female, is the most sensitive part of the male genitals

The shaft of the penis is covered with a loose layer of skin. Male babies are born with a **foreskin** (FOR-skin)—the portion of this layer of skin that extends down over the glans. An operation called **circumcision** (sir-cum-SIZH-un) in which a doctor removes the foreskin is sometimes performed shortly after birth.

Circumcision for some people is a religious custom. You may first have heard or read the word *circumcision* in the Bible. For the Hebrew people circumcision is an important symbol. It is one way by which a boy or man is identified as a Jew. It symbolizes belonging to the people who have entered into a covenant, a special relationship, with God.

Males who have not been **circumcised** (SIR-cum-sized) will find that body oil, dirt, and other particles can collect beneath the foreskin, making it an ideal place for germs to grow and infections to start. For this reason uncircumcised males need to pull back their foreskins and cleanse this part of their body when they are bathing.

It could well be that in ancient times, when water for washing was not always available, circumcision made it easier to stay clean and to prevent genital infections—infections that

# Male Reproductive System
## (external view)

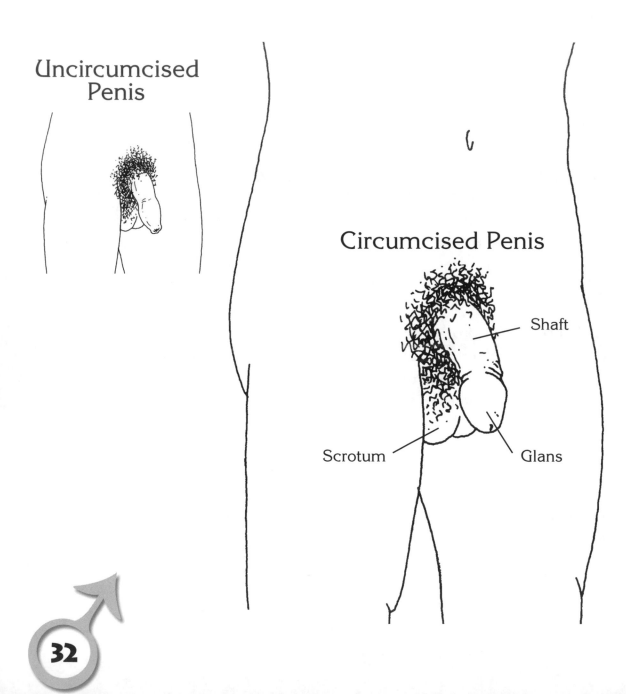

Uncircumcised Penis

Circumcised Penis

Shaft

Scrotum

Glans

could prevent a man from fathering children. Children were believed to be God's way of blessing persons by ensuring that they would be remembered and thus have eternal life. It could be for this reason that circumcision became a part of religious ritual.

Today whether males are circumcised is largely based on cultural and family traditions. Beyond the fact that circumcised and uncircumcised penises look different, they all feel and function the same. Occasionally, a boy or man who was not circumcised in infancy will find that his foreskin is unusually tight and difficult to pull back. In such a case, circumcision may be necessary.

At the center of the glans is the opening to the urethra, which, as in the female, is the tube that allows urine to drain from the bladder. However, you will discover that in males, the urethra is also part of the reproductive system.

The second main part of the male genitals is the **scrotum** (SKRO-tum), the pouch of skin located beneath the penis. Inside the scrotum are the two **testicles** (TESS-tih-kuhls) or **testes** (TESS-tees), egg-shaped organs in which the male reproductive cells or **sperm** and male **hormones** (HOR-mohns) are produced. (An explanation of hormones will follow in Chapter 3.) Attached to each testicle is a small muscle that acts as a thermostat, keeping the testicles at the proper temperature for the production of sperm.

Cold causes the scrotum to contract and the muscles to draw the testicles up to keep them warm. Heat (the weather outside the body or a fever inside the body) causes the muscles to relax, allowing the testicles to hang away from the body.

33

# The Inside Story: Females

The internal sex organs are the organs inside our bodies that identify us as female or male and that make reproduction possible. In females the first organ we come to is the vagina, an elastic, muscular passageway that leads to the other internal sex organs. The vagina, which looks much like a deflated balloon, is three to five inches long when fully developed but can stretch to receive the erect male penis during sexual intercourse or to allow a baby to travel out of the mother's body during childbirth.

The vagina connects to the **uterus** (YOO-tuhr-us) or **womb** (WOOM), a hollow organ located inside the lower abdomen. The uterus, shaped like a light bulb or an upside-down pear, is usually no bigger than a closed fist, but during **pregnancy** (PREG-nun-see) it stretches to accommodate the baby growing inside. The lining of the uterus is called the **endometrium** (ehn-doh-MEE-tree-uhm). The lower part of the uterus that extends into the vagina is called the **cervix** (SER-viks).

**Fallopian** (fuh-LOH-pee-uhn) **tubes**, about four inches long and as thick as a strand of cooked spaghetti, branch out from either side of the upper part of the uterus. At the fringe-like ends of the fallopian tubes are the **ovaries** (OH-vuh-reez), two almond-sized organs located a little lower than the waist. Stored in the ovaries are thousands of **ova** (OH-vah), or female reproductive cells. The ovaries also produce female hormones—chemical substances that will be mentioned later.

# Female Reproductive System
## (internal view)

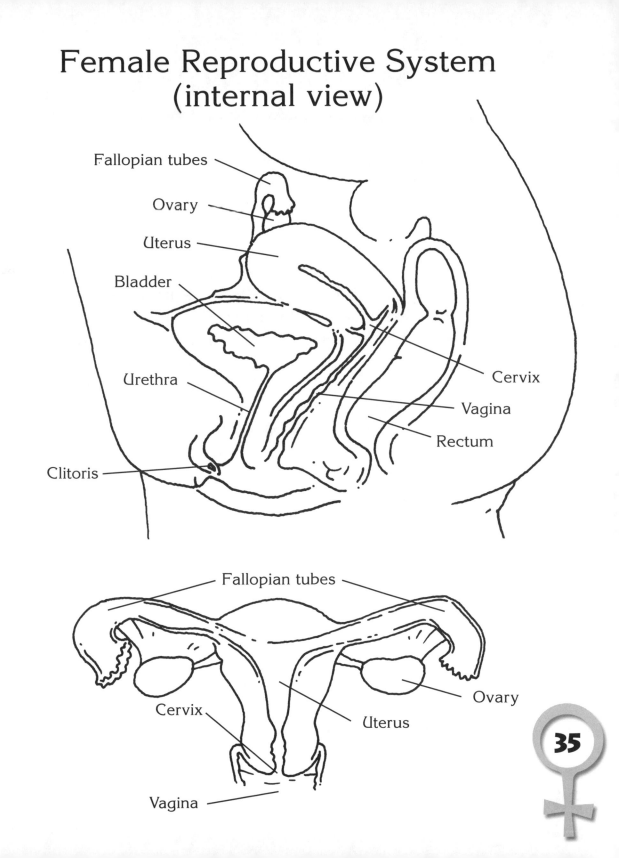

Fallopian tubes

Ovary

Uterus

Bladder

Urethra

Clitoris

Cervix

Vagina

Rectum

Fallopian tubes

Ovary

Cervix

Uterus

Vagina

35

# The Inside Story: Males

**W**e've already mentioned the testicles or testes, two egg-shaped organs located in the scrotum that produce sperm and male hormones. The testicles are made up of about 250 little compartments, and each compartment contains tiny, thread-like tubes. Attached to the back of each testicle is an **epididymis** (ep-uh-DID-uh-mis), another mass of tiny tubes. The sperm produced in the testicles mature during the four to six weeks it takes for them to travel through the epididymis.

Leading up from the epididymis is a **vas deferens** (VAZ DEHF-uhr-uhnz) or sperm duct, a tube 14 to 18 inches long that loops up over the bladder. At the end of the vas deferens is the **ampulla** (am-POOL-uh), a widened portion that serves as the sperm storage area. At the lower part of the ampulla, the **seminal vesicles** (SEM-uh-nuhl VESS-ih-kuhls) connect to the sperm duct. The seminal vesicles make a whitish fluid called **semen** (SEE-muhn), which is critical to the reproductive process.

The **prostate** (PROSS-tate) **gland** is located beneath the bladder, at the intersection of the ampulla and seminal vesicles. This ring-shaped organ has several tubes running through it, one of which is the vas deferens. The prostate gland adds fluid to the semen. During **ejaculation** (ee-JACK-yoo-LAY-shun), which is when sperm and semen are released from the body, the prostate contracts and pushes the sperm and semen into the urethra. Because the sperm and semen travel out of the body through the urethra, it is part of the male's reproductive system.

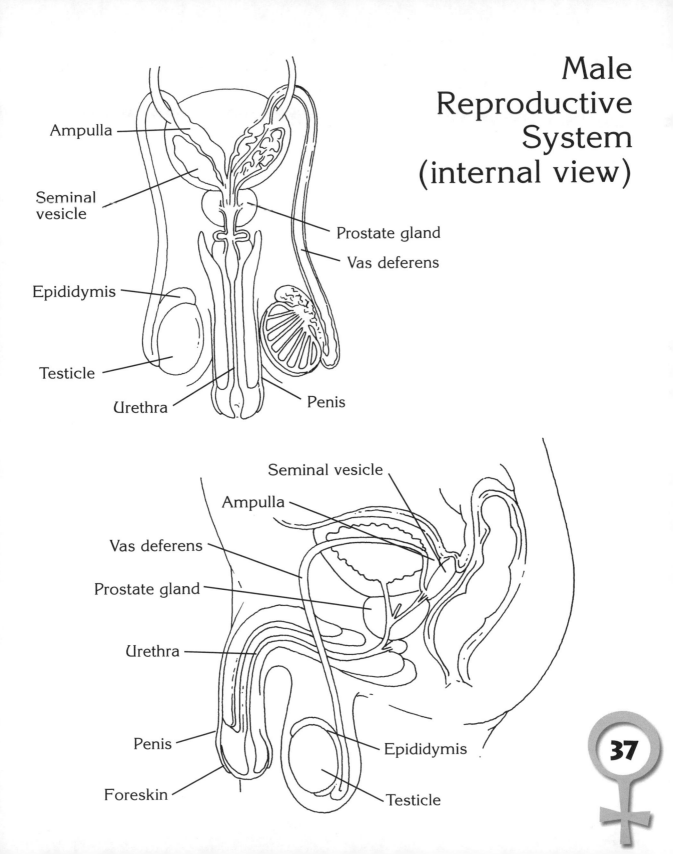

# Male Reproductive System (internal view)

Ampulla

Seminal vesicle

Prostate gland

Vas deferens

Epididymis

Testicle

Urethra

Penis

Seminal vesicle

Ampulla

Vas deferens

Prostate gland

Urethra

Penis

Foreskin

Epididymis

Testicle

That's quite a vocabulary lesson so far. You can expect that learning some of those words will eventually help you feel better about this wonderful body of yours, created in God's own image. With our expanded vocabulary we're ready to learn about what happens to our bodies during that period of amazing change called adolescence. And what happens is nothing short of awesome!

# CHAPTER 3

# Inside and Out: How Change Comes About

Am I Normal?

From Parent to Child

Child to Adult: The Adolescent Female

A New Function, a New Rhythm

Child to Adult: The Adolescent Male

Some Matters for Both
   Girls and Boys

39

# Am I Normal?

For everything there is a season,

and a time for every matter under heaven.

Ecclesiastes 3:1


"When will I start to change?"

"How fast—or how slow—will the changes happen?"

"When will it all be over?"

"Am I normal?"


Let's talk about normal. If you look in the dictionary, you'll find that the word *normal* comes from a Latin word that describes something made using a carpenter's square. A square helps us get our measurements just right when we copy a drawing or pattern.

Normal, therefore, refers to something that fits a pattern. For example, I was taught that 98.6 degrees is the normal temperature of a healthy human body. I have discovered, however, that my body temperature, when I am healthy, is about 96.8 degrees. This is a pattern for me, so 96.8 is my normal body temperature. If my temperature rises to what I was taught was normal, it means that I have a fever. So 98.6 is really an average, rather than what is normal. If you took the temperature of several people, and found the average, it would most likely be about 98.6.

It is probably more helpful to talk about *averages* than about what is or isn't *normal.* If Roslyn has her first period when she is eleven, and Lucy has her first when she is fifteen, the *average* of the two is thirteen. But which one is *normal?* If Gary starts shaving when he is eighteen, and Russ starts when he is fourteen, which of *them* is normal? NOW HEAR THIS! *All* of them are normal, and so are you! Normal, when it comes to how you are growing and developing, is what is right for you.

# From Parent to Child

**W**hen will you start to change? How fast will it happen? When will it all be over? The answers to these questions are locked up in your **chromosomes** (KROH-muh-sohmz). The nuclei (centers) of every cell of your body, like the cells of all plants and animals, contain chromosomes. These tiny rods are how characteristics are passed from parent to offspring. That's called **heredity** (huh-REHD-uh-tee). Chromosomes determine what **gender** (JEN-der) you will be—male or female. Structures called **genes** (JEENZ) are located in specific positions on the chromosomes. They determine what characteristics—such as height and skin, eye, and hair color—you inherited from your parents, from their parents, and so forth.

Genes also determine when you will start, how quickly you will go through, and when you will be finished with **puberty** (PEW-bur-tee). "Puberty" comes from a Latin word that means "to be covered with hair." It refers to the time during which one's body changes from that of a child to that of an adult.

Do some research of your own. Talk with your parents about their experience of puberty. Ask them to show you photos taken as they were growing up. That information, as well as looking at older brothers, sisters, or cousins, might help you predict when and how fast you will mature. Observe persons your age or a bit older. This research will help you imagine what you might have to look forward to. But remember, you will develop at the rate that is right for you. That could be much like your family members and friends, or much different.

Inside your brain, kind of right behind your eyes, is a tiny organ called the **pituitary** (pih-TOO-uh-tare-ee) **gland**. A few years before anyone notices changes taking place in his or her body, the pituitary gland begins manufacturing hormones and sending them into the blood stream. Hormones are chemicals that enable parts of the body to communicate with one another. When the pituitary hormones get to the reproductive glands (ovaries in females and testicles in males), the reproductive glands begin producing hormones of their own, and the adolescent marathon is on!

# Child to Adult: The Adolescent Female

**A**s girls move toward puberty, the pituitary gland produces greater amounts of hormones—stronger signals. These hormones cause the ovaries to make increasing amounts of the female hormone **estrogen** (ESS-truh-juhn). The illustrations on pages 51, 52, and 53 show four girls at eleven, sixteen, and twenty-one years old. Notice the differences between the girls. As our bodies develop, none of them begin or end at the same place, nor do they get from start to finish at the same rate. The one consistent thing is the fact that hormones are responsible for all of the changes that you see taking place as the girls grow older—changes that include the following:

• A growth spurt. This puts many girls ahead of boys their age in terms of height. Boys and girls begin to mature about the same time, but girls generally begin their time of faster growth about two years before boys. Note that not all bones grow at exactly the same rate, which means that arms, legs, and feet may spend some time looking a bit out of proportion to the rest of the body.

43

- The widening of the hips and general change in body shape—literally, from top to bottom.

- The growth of **pubic** (PEW-bick) **hair**—the curly hairs growing in the genital area. For some girls the presence of pubic hair is the first sign that puberty has begun. Some girls notice their first pubic hairs on the edges of the labia. For others the pubic hair begins growing first on the mons. Why pubic hair? Pubic hair functions like eyelashes, preventing dust or dirt particles from irritating sensitive parts of the body.

- The growth of hair in the underarms and the darkening and growth of hair on the legs. We won't get into a detailed discussion about shaving, but the growth of hair in the underarms and on the legs means it's time for a chat with a parent or other trusted adult on the subject. Shaving is one of many cultural or family issues for which there are no general answers. Decision-making starts with conversation.

- The sensitivity and development of the **breasts**. During childhood the breasts are flat, with only the center or **nipple** standing out. During puberty the breasts begin to swell and stand out more, and the nipple and darker area surrounding it, called the **areola** (air-ee-OH-lah), get larger and darker in color. The first sign of change might be the presence of a small, button-like lump or mound. This indicates the development of **milk ducts** (duhkts) inside the breast.

   The breasts are made up of 15 to 25 sections called **lobes**. When a woman has a baby, milk is produced inside the lobes and travels through the milk ducts as the baby sucks on the nipple. Milk is not actually produced until a woman has a baby, but during puberty, a girl's breasts are developing so that she might later be able to breast feed.

# Female Breast

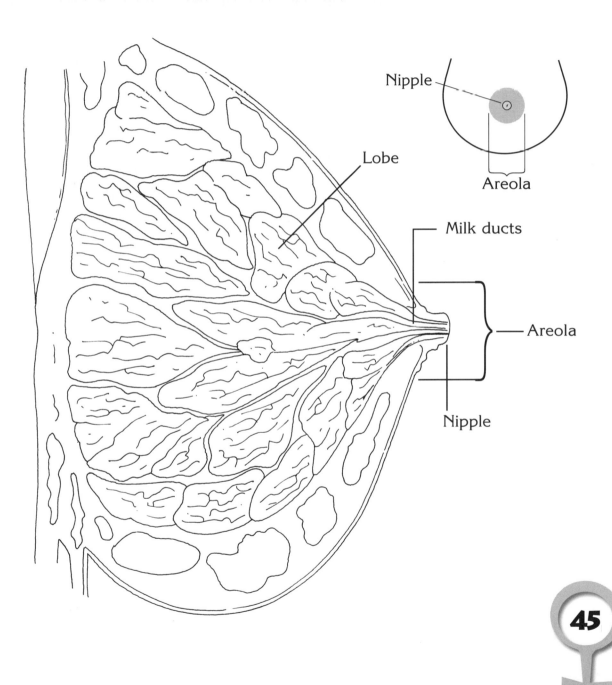

Nipple

Areola

Lobe

Milk ducts

Areola

Nipple

45

Breast development—its starting point, how long it lasts, and how much development occurs—differs greatly among growing girls. Girls whose breasts develop early feel self-conscious. Girls whose breasts develop later feel self-conscious. Such a big deal is made about breasts in the media, girls may begin to think that the size of their breasts makes more of a difference than it actually does. Many of them are concerned about whether they are normal. Remember: *Who's* normal? *You*, that's *who!*

• The need to begin caring for breasts. For now, the big decision is not related to babies and breast feeding, but when or whether to begin wearing a bra. That's one more issue to take up with parents or other adults. While you're talking, be sure to discuss the importance of doing a regular (monthly) **Breast Self-Examination (BSE)** and how to do one. All maturing girls and women need to examine and be familiar with their breasts. Knowledge of their bodies keeps them alert to changes later on that could signal possible breast disease.

The self-exam involves looking at the breasts to be aware of any changes and checking for an irregular discharge from the nipples (not all discharges are a problem). A thorough self-exam also includes feeling the entire breast and the area around the breast, pressing firmly with a circular motion, all the way down to the chest wall. This is best done while lying down. Breasts are normally lumpy, so regular exams are necessary in order to be able to tell the difference between normal lumps and ones that need to be reported to your doctor.

• The changes taking place in and around the vulva. The mons begins to stick out more as this fat tissue thickens. The outer and inner labia darken and become thicker and more wrinkly. Generally, the thickening of the outer labia will eventually cause them to touch. The hymen also grows thicker.

- The increased sensitivity of the genital area. As puberty begins, girls discover new sensations as they explore the **vaginal** (VAJ-uh-nuhl) **area**—especially the clitoris, which grows larger during puberty. The touching or stroking of the genitals is part of the self-discovery process of all girls and boys. This kind of touching is called **masturbation** (MASS-ter-BAY-shun).

As puberty begins, girls find that the nice feelings they had as young children while touching their genitals have been replaced by much stronger feelings. In response to stimulation, there is an increase in the amount of blood flowing to the genital area, causing the clitoris to become larger or erect. At puberty, masturbation may lead to the intense and pleasant pulsing of muscles called an **orgasm** (OR-gaz-uhm). More will be said about masturbation in Chapter 5.

- The growth of the uterus. It still doesn't get very large, but the walls become thicker.

- The beginning of **menstruation** (men-STRAY-shun).

# A New Function, a New Rhythm

**A** cycle is something that happens again and again. Like the beat to your favorite song, the female body has its own rhythm or cycle: the **menstrual** (MEN-struhl) **cycle**. The estrogen produced by the ovaries signals the body when it's time to "catch the beat." The signal comes most often between the ages of ten and fifteen, but can come earlier or later.

A girl is born with hundreds of thousands of ova in her ovaries. Each **ovum** (OH-vum—the singular of ova), about the size of the point on a sharp pencil, is inside a tiny sac called a **follicle** (FALL-uh-kuhl). As puberty begins, some of the folli-

47

cles and their ova begin to change and mature, or ripen, and move from the center of the ovary toward the surface.

As a follicle reaches the surface, it presses on the outer covering of the ovary, which causes a tiny blister-like bubble to form. When the blister bursts open, the ovum is released from the ovary. This process, called **ovulation** (ah-vyue-LAY-shun), happens about once a month or every 28 days.

For the first year or two (sometimes longer) after they begin menstruating, many girls find that their periods are very irregular. They could start their period only 20 days after the beginning of their last cycle, or could go a number of months between periods. The periods tend to become more regular as a girl gets older.

The ovaries generally take turns ovulating—the right ovary one month, and the left ovary the next. Once the ovum has been released from the ovary, the fringed end of the fallopian tube on that side reaches out like fingers to grasp the ovum and draw it into the tube. Tiny hairs called **cilia** (SILL-ee-uh) then propel the ovum through the four-inch-long tube at the record-breaking rate of about one inch per day! (Remember that the ovum is the size of a pencil point, so traveling an inch in a day is a bigger deal than it might first seem.)

Prior to ovulation, the lining of the uterus (the endometrium) doubles in thickness with new blood vessels and spongy tissue—all rich with nutrients. If the ovum traveling through the fallopian tube is fertilized by a male reproductive cell (sperm), the fertilized ovum implants in the endometrium, where it is nourished, and pregnancy begins.

More often than not, fertilization does not take place. When the ovum is not fertilized, the body tells itself, *There's no fertilized ovum in here looking for a place to grow, so I don't need this extra lining in my uterus.* A couple of weeks after ovulation, the uterus sheds its lining as a bloody discharge that passes through the vagina and out of the body. This process is menstruation, often referred to as a **menstrual period** or simply a **period**. The length of the period varies from person to person, but typically lasts two to seven days.

During menstruation a girl or woman protects her clothing by using a feminine hygiene product—either a cotton-like pad called a **sanitary napkin**, or a small, tightly wrapped cylinder of cotton-like material called a **tampon** (TAM-pahn). The sanitary napkin or pad is fastened to the inside of the underpants by adhesive strips and covers the vulva. The tampon is inserted into the vagina using an applicator that comes with the tampon. Both items absorb the menstrual discharge and are replaced as needed. As menstrual flow subsides, many girls and women wear a thin pantyliner or a light day's pad with a bottom layer of plastic. This extra precaution ensures protection should there be a continued light discharge.

When changing sanitary napkins or tampons, girls may notice clumps of tissue as well as blood. Remember that the thickened lining of the uterus is being discharged, which means that more than blood is leaving the body. How much is discharged? While it often seems like more, only one-fourth to three-fourths of a cup dribbles out during the period.

Bathing and washing are especially important during menstruation. Many girls and women find that they perspire more at this time and that their perspiration has a stronger odor. Bathing frequently and paying particular attention to the genital area; using deodorant or antiperspirant under the arms; and changing the pad or tampon regularly generally lessen the problem.

Girls usually have little difficulty with menstruation. They can bathe, take part in sports, and continue their normal activities. Some girls, however, may experience abdominal cramping, pain in the legs or back, or headaches. An aspirin substitute such as ibuprofen or acetaminophen usually

49

relieves the temporary discomfort, as does the use of a heating pad. If she experiences a lot of discomfort, a girl should ask the advice of her physician.

Menstruation is normal, but it's not always convenient. Because it is difficult to know exactly when the menstrual period will start, many girls prepare by keeping a sanitary pad or tampon in their purses or school lockers. Restrooms and school nurses' offices often have a supply available as well.

*What do I do if I start my period at school and my teacher's a man?* Male teachers, as well as females, understand that menstruation is a part of every girl's life. A simple, direct "I need to go to the nurse's office" or "I need to go to the restroom" should take care of it. Teachers generally understand without further question.

There are some signs that can indicate a period is about to begin. Pubic hair and breast development generally come before the first period. Some girls will notice a discharge from their vaginas—not blood, but a thick fluid. This fluid is just how the body keeps the uterus and vagina clean. Sometimes the body retains water, making the girl feel "bloated."

Girls and boys: Talk with your female relatives about their first periods and about how they felt just before it happened. It's one of those events that most women remember. Their responses—especially if there seems to be a pattern—may be your best clue as to when you will have your first period if you are a girl, and may make you more aware and more sensitive if you are a boy.

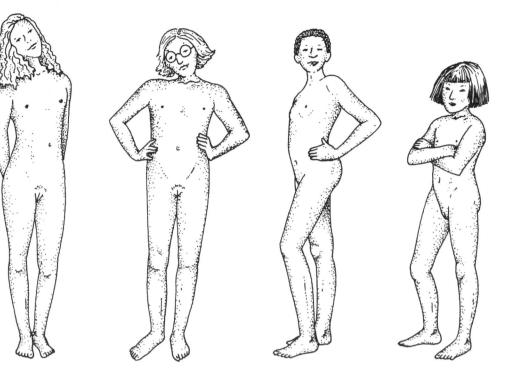

# Around 11 Years Old

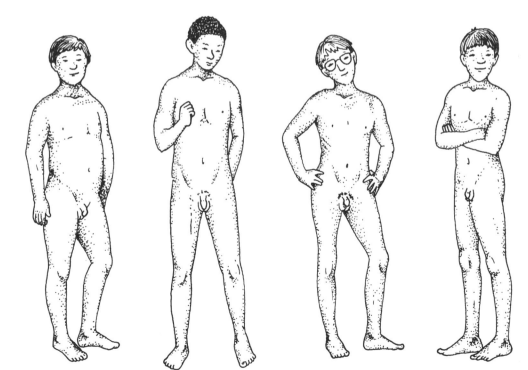

51

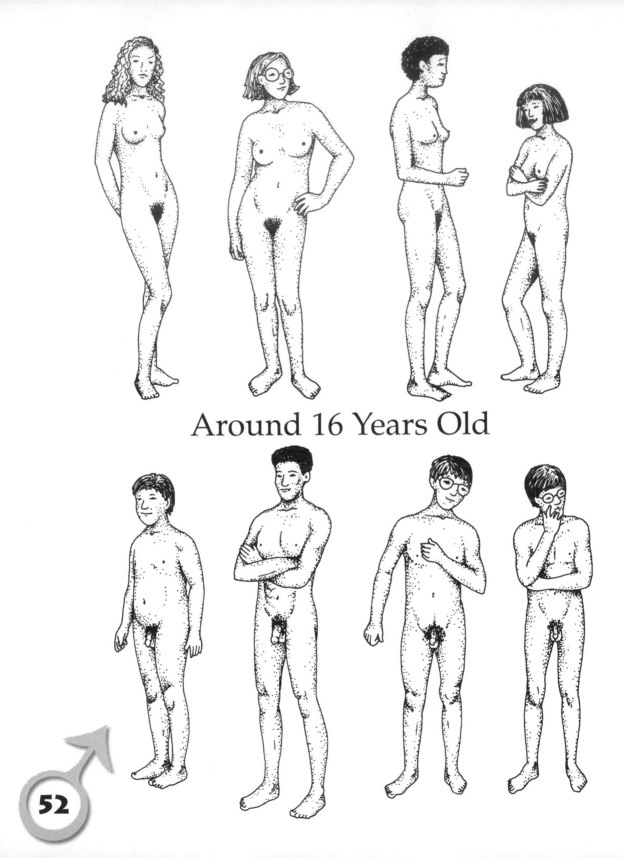

# Around 16 Years Old

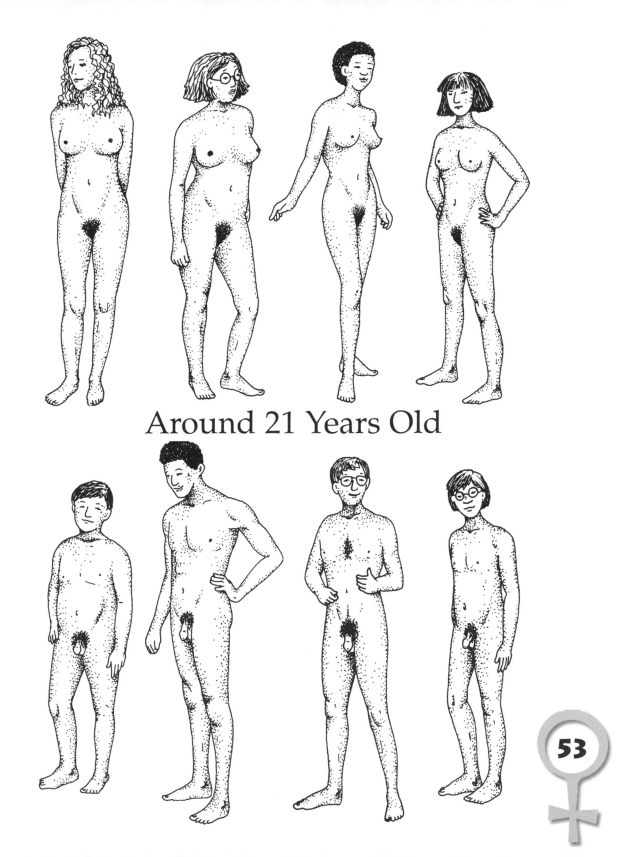

Around 21 Years Old

53

# Child to Adult: The Adolescent Male

**N**otice the differences between the boys illustrated on pages 51, 52, and 53. When it comes to puberty, every boy's body (just like every girl's body) is unique. At the time that is right for the individual, the pituitary gland sends its hormone signals to the testicles, instructing them to produce more of the male hormone **testosterone** (tess-TOSS-tuh-rone). The changes caused by the testosterone are often noticed at about eleven or twelve years old, but can come a year or more before or a year or more after this age. Some of these changes are as follows:

• The testicles and scrotum grow larger, and the scrotum darkens in color. This is often the first sign that a boy has entered puberty. As development continues, one testicle (generally the left one) begins to hang lower than the other. This is the body's way of protecting two very sensitive organs from being painfully pressed together between the legs, especially when boys or men are being very active.

• The need increases to care for the testicles. The athletic supporters (jock straps) or cup protectors that boys and men wear when involved in athletics protect the testicles by holding them close to the body. But there is another way in which growing boys and adult men need to care for their bodies—something called a **Testicular** (tess-TIC-yuh-luhr) **Self-Examination** or **TSE**.

The TSE is best done in the shower when the scrotum is warm and relaxed. Each testicle is rolled between the thumb and first three fingers, and the entire surface of the testicles is checked for lumps or irregularities. The sperm ducts and epididymis, connected to the testicles, don't count as irregularities. The only way to know when a change has taken place in the testicles that needs to be reported to a doctor is by being familiar with these two organs through a regular (monthly is best) TSE. It's very unusual for teenagers and young men to get cancer, but when they do, it's often testicular.

• The penis grows larger. First it grows longer and then begins to get wider. The head of the penis (glans) is more noticeable as being distinct from the shaft. Like the scrotum, the penis darkens in color. Since genital size is a concern for many boys (and many men), the following information might help. Grown men's testicles are usually about one and three-fourth inches long. Penises are usually between three and one-fourth and four and one-fourth inches long when soft or limp, and usually between five and seven inches long when hard or **erect** (ih-REKT). I emphasize usually because we are talking about what is average, not about what is normal or what should be.

It would be foolish to tell you that the size of one's penis doesn't make any difference. If that was the case, we wouldn't be discussing it. While penis size doesn't make a difference in how masculine you are or what kind of a husband or father you will be, it can make a difference in how you feel about yourself. It's not unusual for older boys with larger penises to make fun of younger boys with smaller penises. I'd suggest right now, well before you know how your body will turn out as a result of this whole puberty process, that you remind yourself on a regular basis that you are God's outstanding creation—just the way you are and just the way you will be.

• Hair begins to grow in the pubic area. Pubic hair generally shows up first at the base of the penis and then on the scro-

tum. The first hairs are long and slightly curly, then they become darker, curlier, and cover more territory.

• Hair begins to grow in the underarms and on the face, and hair on the rest of the body begins to get thicker and darker. This process continues for some boys into their early twenties. Boys are often anxious to shave for the first time— although they wouldn't want anyone to know that. It's one of those informal rites of passage. Some twelve-year-olds will find that they need or want to begin shaving—upper lips and sideburns seem to be the first targets. Others won't need to start until sixteen, seventeen, or even later. Having a parent or other adult to talk with and offer advice will be a big help, both with regards to how you're feeling and how to get the job done when you're ready.

• The voice begins to deepen, but not without its share of cracks and squeaks on the way down. The voice box is growing, and the muscles that are responsible for producing sound need to be retrained. In the meantime don't "force" your voice. Be sure to breathe before you speak. This won't eliminate the squeaks and cracks, but may minimize them.

• Over fifty percent of all boys experience some swelling and tenderness of the breasts during puberty. The nipples may get a bit larger, the ring of colored flesh around the nipple may get wider and darker, and many boys notice a rather flat, button-like lump under one or both nipples. This is neither a sign of disease nor an indication that one is turning into a girl! It is one of the ways in which boys' bodies react to hormones. Male and female hormones are present in all persons. Once the amount of hormones becomes balanced, this condition passes.

This is probably a good time to remind you to be sensitive to what girls are going through regarding breast development, and NEVER to tease girls about their breasts.

• Boys experience a growth spurt. Boys begin to catch up and generally exceed the girls in height. They may gain as much as 25 pounds in a single year.

• Shoulders broaden and body shape changes, largely due to the increase in the size and number of muscle cells.

• Boys begin to experience more frequent **erections** (ee-RECK-shunz). Most of the time the penis is soft or limp. Sometimes, though, as a result of some type of stimulation, blood rushes into the penis, filling tiny hollow sacs inside the shaft. Muscles at the base of the penis tighten and keep the blood from flowing back into the body. This causes the penis to become larger, firmer, and to stand out from the body—sometimes straight up, sometimes straight out, sometimes somewhere in between. Everyone's angle is a little different. This is an erection, and it occurs in males of all ages, even before birth.

The stimulation that leads to an erection can be a matter of touching the genitals, being rubbed by tight clothing, needing to urinate, feeling the vibrations of a car or bus that needs new shock absorbers, having thoughts about sex, or simply being close to a person for whom one has special feelings. Boys and men experience erections several times while they are asleep and often awaken with an erection.

Sometimes erections happen with no obvious explanation. A boy might be thinking of just about anything and suddenly find himself with an erection. Growing minds are making connections between experiences and feelings. Do you know how a cool breeze causes goose bumps to automatically

57

appear on your arms? how sounds—a song you enjoy listening to, an unexpected scream, or fingernails scratching across a chalkboard—can cause an automatic reaction? Sometimes goose bumps or other reactions happen as we just think of these kinds of things.

Adolescents react more strongly than children to what they see, hear, smell, taste, feel, and think. You used to look at a rock and see a rock. Now you might see that same rock, be reminded of someplace special you once visited, and begin to have some of the same feelings you had during that visit. Your mind brings those feelings back automatically. Such connections could be the reason behind the for-no-reason erections that boys experience more frequently during puberty.

Erections usually aren't noticed by anyone else and don't last forever. Should a boy find himself with an erection at a time when someone might notice it—whether that be in the locker room or in the middle of giving a report in front of the history class—he needs to remember that what he is experiencing is perfectly normal. A boy might try taking several deep breaths and focusing his attention on something other than the erection. Since there's nothing wrong with him or with what he's doing, there's no need to go to extremes to try to cover up and hide. Some boys cope by wearing baggy pants and long shirts. Some carry their books in such a way as to conceal their erection. The good news is that as a boy moves out of adolescence and into adulthood, hormones calm down and erections become less of a problem.

You have probably heard about drugs that men take when they are having just the opposite problem—when they can't have an erection and are unable to have sexual intercourse. However, men who don't need these drugs also are taking them out of curiosity or thinking that their enjoyment of intercourse will be increased. Not knowing what the long-term effects of these relatively new drugs could be, we think this is a bad idea.

• Boys experience their first ejaculation. Hormones have stimulated the body to begin producing the sperm and semen already mentioned. Ejaculation refers to what happens when the mixture of sperm and semen is pushed from the seminal vesicles into the urethra. As muscles automatically give a strong squeeze, the fluid is squirted out of the penis. This ejaculation is accompanied by an orgasm which, as with girls, refers to very pleasant pulsing feelings in the genital area.

The first ejaculation happens for many boys somewhere around fourteen years of age, although it is perfectly normal for it to happen before or after this time. Two out of three boys experience their first ejaculation during masturbation. Masturbation is the deliberate touching or stroking of one's

sex organs. As boys develop, their sex organs become more sensitive, and masturbation produces very strong and pleasant sensations. While masturbation does not always end in orgasm and ejaculation, once a boy's body has begun producing sperm, he'll usually ejaculate if he masturbates long enough. We'll discuss this more in Chapter 5.

One out of three boys has his first ejaculation while he is asleep. This is called a **nocturnal emission** (nock-TER-nul ee-MISH-uhn), or wet dream. It happens because the seminal vesicles are full of semen, and the mind is able during sleep to produce the kind of stimulation that leads to an orgasm. No need to worry! This is simply part of how God has designed the male body to relieve itself of sexual tension and excess semen.

How often do wet dreams happen? That varies greatly from one boy to the next. Some boys never have them. It's OK if they do and OK if they don't. Just know that they are a possibility. If you are a boy and you awaken and find a damp spot on your pajamas or sheets, you'll know what happened. When semen dries, it can discolor fabric and leave it a little stiff, so you may prefer to have your pajamas and sheets washed. Don't worry. Parents understand.

# Some Matters for Both Girls & Boys

We are created by God:
some of us female,
some of us male,
each of us special,
each of us sexual,
each of us growing at our own unique pace.

**M**any young people like you wonder and worry about whether their bodies are "on schedule" when it comes to physical development. We have already made reference to the illustrations on pages 51, 52, and 53 showing four girls and four boys when they are around eleven, sixteen, and twenty-one years of age. As you look at these illustrations, note that bodies come in all different types at all ages.

Some young people begin to look quite mature in their mid-teens. For some this happens a few years earlier, and for others it happens a few years later. Remember that everyone is different. With all of the variety there is among bodies in God's world, you fit in quite nicely! What a fantastic creation you are!

About the time that you begin to grow underarm hair, or even before, you may notice that your underarms have begun to perspire more and that the odor has changed. This may be true for other parts of your body—your hands, feet, and genitals—as well. Again, these are effects of the hormones at work in your body. Regular bathing or showering and changing clothing may take care of the situation, although you may find that the use of a deodorant or antiperspirant makes you more comfortable.

Oily skin and **acne** (ACK-nee) or pimples is another condition that is common to young people who are going through puberty. Yes, this can be blamed on the hormones too! But rather than just laying blame, let's be practical and consider what to do about acne.

There is no guaranteed cure for the situation, but washing your hair regularly and washing your face, shoulders, back, and upper chest with a non-abrasive soap twice a day may help by cleansing those areas of excess oils. Sometimes a medication containing benzoyl peroxide may be used. If you should be worried that acne is becoming a problem for you, talk with your physician about it.

All of these phenomena can be traced to the work of that special timing mechanism, the pituitary gland, and to the hormone signals it is sending through your body right this very minute. Pretty amazing stuff, wouldn't you say? It's all normal—and so, by the way, are you!

# CHAPTER  4

# Being Female, Being Male, Being You

The Story of Adam and Eve

Quit Looking at Me!

Two New Words

Stereotypes

Celebrate Yourself!

Building Bridges

Friends: Paula and Tiffany

Friends: Carlos and Tim

Friends: Susan and Ronny

Feminine and Masculine

Possibilities—Open to All

63

# The Story of Adam and Eve

The story of Adam and Eve is a story of people growing up. Long before it was written down, this tale was passed from one generation to the next by storytellers. Reading the story in Genesis 2:15-25, I hear the storyteller chuckle a bit while explaining God's solution to Adam's need for companionship. Animals!

In the days before Eve, Adam was feeling lonely. So God provided him with pets—lots of pets! God said to Adam, "These ought to make you feel better, Adam. How about some names

for these critters?" Naming the animals kept Adam busy for a while, but it wasn't long before God (and Adam) realized that, nice as the animals were, they didn't meet Adam's need for a partner.

Plan B: God created another human being. The rib business in the story means that Eve was made out of the same stuff as Adam. But even though they had things like ribs in common, Eve was still a different kind of human—a female kind. Perhaps that's what made Eve so suitable as a partner for Adam! They enjoyed the ways they were the same and also enjoyed discovering and exploring the many ways in which they were different.

The Bible says that "the man and his wife were both naked, and were not ashamed" (Genesis 2:25). Their differences were no problem to them. They were each comfortable with themselves and with the other. No big deal.

Unfortunately Adam and Eve didn't stay comfortable. They made some poor decisions, and their relationship with God and with each other began to fall apart. They began looking for leaves to cover the most obvious of their differences—their bodies. As their relationship with God broke down, their differences became an embarrassment to them.

# Quit Looking at Me!

It started without warning.

"Quit looking at me!" Pete shouted at his younger brother.

"I wasn't!"

"Mom, make him stop!"

"Stop what?" Mom asked as she came in the room to find out what the shouting was all about.

"Looking at me like that."

"Like what?" she asked.

"I don't know. He's just always looking at me."

While that conversation might not make much sense, it's one you recognize, isn't it? You probably understand exactly how Pete felt. Like many girls and boys your age, you sometimes feel as though everyone is looking at you, watching what you are doing, grading your appearance, and rating your behavior. You feel that people are expecting you to look, to sound, to dress, and to grow a certain way. Even when people aren't watching, you feel as though they are. These are anxious feelings because there is no way that you or anyone else can meet all those expectations.

If the young people I know had their way, everyone would look about the same. No one would be the tallest or the shortest, the best- or worst-dressed, the most or least popular. Among the girls, no one would have the most- or the least-developed breasts. No one would be the first or last to have her period. Among the boys, no one would have the greatest or the least amount of body hair or be the first or last to have his voice change. Everyone would be the same. No one would stand out in the crowd.

Would that kind of sameness take some of the pressure off of you? Would sameness make everything fair? Maybe the unfairness is the "rule" that everyone has to look or be the same in order to eliminate the differences between people.

# Two New Words

As the growth process causes the differences among boys, among girls, and between girls and boys to become more and more obvious, it's easy for young people to begin moving further and further apart from each other. Comparing themselves to others, they decide who is better. That's called competition. Competition calls for winners and losers.

Maybe **intimacy** (IN-tuh-muh-see) isn't a new word to you. If you have heard it, you might have heard it used to name the sexual behaviors that sometimes go on between men and women. But intimacy is more than close contact between bodies. Intimacy means a close friendship between people. Intimacy happens when people take the time to get to know each other's likes, dislikes, hopes, and fears; when they learn to accept one another just as they are. Intimacy is something that can happen between any two people who are willing to work at it.

Intimacy puts an end to competition. The object of intimacy is not to decide who is best, but to simply enjoy being together and getting to know one another. Think about the people with whom you feel most comfortable. Who are the people with whom you can just be yourself and not worry about who's watching you or how you compare? Who are the persons with whom you feel OK admitting your mistakes and your weaknesses? These are the people with whom you are building intimacy.

Intimacy can be a scary thing because it exposes our **vulnerability** (VUHL-ner-uh-BILL-uh-tee). You know about Superman and kryptonite, don't you? Just like Superman, we all have our vulnerabilities—obstacles we can't overcome, things we either can't do or will never do well. There are some things we can never be. Boys can't be girls or know what it feels like to be a girl. Girls can't be boys or know what it feels like to be a boy. There are some things that we can only understand or experience by getting close to other people. These are some of our vulnerabilities.

The key to intimacy is honesty. Being honest about our vulnerabilities can help make a relationship strong. Girls don't have to compete with one another to prove who is the best girl. Boys don't have to compete with one another to prove who is the best boy. Girls and boys don't have to compete with each other to prove that either girls or boys are best. Intimacy is accepting and enjoying people for who they are. You don't have to be like everyone else. You don't have to be the best. Just be yourself!

# Stereotypes

Originally, "**stereotype**" (STAIR-ee-uh-type) was the name for a metal printing plate used to print words or pictures over and over again. Today we use that same word to describe how people of a particular group are sometimes expected to look, or behave, or think. Stereotypes are like shadows. Shadows are just outlines of what is really there.

The shadow of one person can be pretty much like the shadow of another person. Everyone ends up looking pretty much the same.

A stereotype of males might suggest that all men are young, muscular, tall, and handsome. They wear the right clothes, have their hair styled the right way, say the right things, drive the right car, and fall in love with the right woman. A stereotype of females might try to convince us that all women are beautiful, young, and have well-shaped bodies. They always wear just the right shade of nail polish, lipstick, and eye makeup. They are never seen in the same outfit twice in one month. They fall in love with the right man, and they can't wait to be mothers.

Even though these stereotypes do not describe all men or all women—or even *most* of them—there are persons spending millions of dollars on advertising every year to convince us that everyone ought to fit these stereotypes. Their goal is to convince us that their product is just what we need to fit the stereotype!

# Celebrate Yourself!

**F**reedom is an idea that relates to all we have been talking about. Stereotypes confine people by telling them what they should and shouldn't be. Breaking stereotypes sets people free—free to be who they are and free to *celebrate* who they are. You may *want* to be like someone else, but you don't *have* to be like anyone else. You can feel great about being who you are!

Let's go a step further. Feeling good about yourself is something you have the right and the responsibility to do. A story from the life of Jesus might help us understand.

**69**

Jesus was once approached by a scribe (a teacher of religious law) who asked him, "Which commandment is the first of all?" Jesus answered the question by quoting from the Book of Deuteronomy. "Hear, O Israel!" Jesus said. "The Lord our God, the Lord is one; you shall love the Lord your God with all your heart, and with all your soul, and with all your mind, and with all your strength."

Jesus didn't stop there. He took what he considered to be the most important commandment and paired it with a second one: "You shall love your neighbor as yourself," Jesus said to the scribe. "There is no other commandment greater than these" (from Mark 12:28-31).

As you grow in your ability to understand what's going on around you, you are discovering that your feelings about God, about other people, and about yourself are all connected. If you aren't feeling good about yourself, it's pretty tough to put your whole self—heart, soul, mind, and strength—into loving God. If you haven't learned to love yourself, to say to yourself, *Hey! I'm OK just the way I am*, you're going to have a tough time loving your neighbor. Remember that neighbor can refer to anybody—not just the person who lives next door, or even the person who is like you in many ways.

If you're a girl, the kind of neighbor Jesus talks about could very well be a boy. And if you're a boy, it might be a girl.

# Building Bridges

**W**hen you feel good about yourself—including feeling good about your growing and changing body—you find lots of energy and enthusiasm to give to loving God and to loving neighbor. You're all set to get at the task of building bridges—building intimacy—between people and between people and God. These good feelings about yourself have a lot to do with how you see yourself as a female or as a male. They don't always happen automatically. They have to be worked at. I can't think of more important work for girls and boys like you to be doing.

Bridge-building begins by learning about yourself. You're learning to call the parts and functions of your body by their proper names. You're learning to recognize some of the slang terms that are used to describe the same parts and functions. You don't have to use the slang terms, but you'll feel better if you know what they refer to. It's usually best to have a bit more information on hand than what you actually need.

Your expanded vocabulary will make it easier for you to talk to others about the thoughts and feelings you have about yourself. You'll also be able to better understand when others express their thoughts and feelings. You are building bridges with words, information, and understandings that you have in common with other persons.

It is important that girls build bridges with other girls. There are some things that only another girl can completely understand. Boys need to build bridges with other boys. Many people live with the stereotype that boys and men never share their feelings, that they can work out all of their problems on their own. Not so! Boys need to practice talking to each other about their feelings.

Girls and boys need to get to know each other by talking to each other. This particular kind of bridge-building can prepare people for the possibility of being married someday. But whether or not they choose to be married, boys and girls need to build bridges between each other while they are young, simply because they live in a world where people come in two genders! The following stories may help you to see how important bridge-building can be.

# Friends: Paula and Tiffany

**P**aula and Tiffany had a problem! As their bodies began to change, they found that their nipples were becoming tender and were being irritated by the rubbing of their clothing. But their breasts hadn't developed much—at least they hadn't gotten that much larger, and they were sure that their mothers wouldn't see the need for them to begin wearing bras.

They suffered separately for a while. Finally, Paula timidly mentioned the situation to Tiffany. Both were relieved to know that they weren't alone with the problem.

"I can't believe you've been going through the same thing!" Together they came up with a plan. "If one of us can get her mother to agree to the bra, the other's mother is sure to go along with the idea!" They decided that at 5 o'clock they

would both go to their mothers and tell them that they needed bras.

To their amazement both mothers understood and agreed
to take them shopping that evening for their first bras. Let's
give those mothers some credit for remembering back to
when they experienced the same thing. But let's also recognize two smart friends who managed to put their feelings into
words and who tackled their problem together!

# Friends: Carlos and Tim

**T**hey had been buddies since third grade, so Tim could
tell something was wrong with his friend Carlos. Though
Carlos tended to be quiet, for the past three days he had been
almost silent. Hearing some boys talking after school, Tim
finally figured out what was bothering Carlos.

Carlos and three other boys had a backyard sleepout the
weekend before—complete with a campfire. First they told all
the ghost stories they knew and then all the dirty jokes. Each
of the boys tried to top the others either by being more scary
or by impressing them with their knowledge about sex.

One of them started an "I'll show you mine if you show me
yours" kind of thing, daring them to expose their genitals. No
one wanted the others to think he was a "chicken," so they all
went along with the dare. Somehow the story got out, and
after three days it was hard to say who had heard about it or
what story they had heard.

Tim's first thought was that he would be better off to avoid
Carlos. But he thought again. Tim had learned that in a situation like this, he felt better after spending some time talking
to God about it. That's what he did. The next afternoon he

73

cornered Carlos.

"Want to talk?" asked Tim.

"About what?" Carlos replied.

"Friday night."

Carlos turned a bright red. "You heard?"

"Yeah."

Carlos started to run, but Tim grabbed his arm and stopped him. "Do you think you're the first one to do something like that?"

"I don't know. It was so stupid!" said Carlos.

"Maybe," Tim answered.

"Still want to be my friend?" asked Carlos.

"Still want to be mine?" asked Tim. Carlos looked puzzled as Tim blushed, took a deep breath, and continued. "Like I said, do you think you're the first one to do something like that?" Tim talked a little about his own experience and feelings. Carlos began to relax. Tim was some special friend—the kind of friend who helps a person get through the tough parts of growing up.

# Friends: Susan and Ronny

"**V**alerie Taylor likes you!" shouted Susan to Ronny as he headed toward home. Ronny turned, gave her a dirty look, and kept going.

"Ronny, did you hear me? I said Val–"

"Heard you?" he interrupted. "The whole neighborhood heard you!"

"Sorry. Well, do you like her?"

"Like who?"

"Valerie Taylor! You said you heard me!"

"Me and everyone within five blocks of here."

"You still didn't answer me."

"I don't plan to."

"You make me so angry!" said Susan.

"You embarrass me," Ronny replied.

"I didn't think you could embarrass."

"Surprise!"

Susan thought for a moment. "I am sorry, Ronny. I guess I wasn't thinking."

I don't know where Valerie Taylor stands, but if Ronny and Susan can keep talking and listening and can be more sensitive to each other, they might even become friends!

# Feminine and Masculine

**Y**ou're beginning to have a better understanding of your body and of others' bodies as well. You're also working on your understanding of what it means to be **feminine** (FEHM-uh-nin) and **masculine** (MASS-kyuh-lin). So are Martin and Randy, two twelve-year-olds with heads full of stereotypes as to what twelve-year-old boys ought to look like. They're in the locker room at the YMCA.

As they stand under the showers, Martin is aware that his body hasn't started to develop yet—at least not on the outside where others can see. (By the way, Martin isn't the only one making such observations! It's just one of the things that growing boys and girls do.) Martin hasn't started to sprout any hair under his arms or around his genitals—quite normal for his age. Randy, on the other hand, is showing some of the signs of puberty, including the start of a moustache—also quite normal. Does one of these boys represent the stereotype for all boys their age?

Cindy and Dawn, two girls at a slumber party, have had their minds filled with stereotypes too. Cindy was ten years old when she had her first period. At twelve she is one of the girls whose breasts are well-developed. Dawn is three months older than Cindy but still hasn't had her first period and hasn't started wearing a bra yet. Do either Dawn or Cindy represent the stereotype for all twelve-year-old girls? Is one of these girls more feminine than the other?

People often affirm the appearance or the behavior of young girls by making comments such as, "Isn't she a little lady!" The same happens to young boys with comments like,

"He's all boy!" People may mean well, but they aren't always helpful. Little girls are little girls—not ladies. It's not fair to expect a little girl to be a lady and to miss being a little girl. Boys don't come half boy and half salamander. But people have a picture in their minds—a stereotype—of what girls and boys should be like. When they see things in girls and boys that match their mental pictures, they point these things out. What happens then? Boys and girls grow up thinking that all boys should be alike and that all girls should be alike. That's neither true nor fair.

When it comes to gender, you're either male or female; you're either a boy or a girl. There's nothing mysterious or uncertain about it. Gender is not something you have by degrees. You can't be more girl or less girl, or more boy or less boy, than someone else. Chapter 3 already mentioned chromosomes, and Chapter 5 will explain a bit more how gender is determined. What you need to know in this chapter is that you are either male or female—*all* male or *all* female.

Feminine is something different. So is masculine. They have nothing to do with how early you develop, how late you develop, or how large or how small parts of your body are. Femininity is how a person chooses to express her understanding of what it means to be female. Masculinity is how a person chooses to express his understanding of what it means to be male. Different persons express themselves in different ways. Much of that is determined by the culture in which we are raised. Some of us will choose to express our femaleness or maleness in traditional ways. That's fine! Some of us will choose not to be limited by what people have considered feminine and masculine in the past. That's fine too!

**77**

# Possibilities—Open to All

**T**oday girls and boys have similar dreams and share many of the same possibilities. Girls and boys both have an opportunity to receive an education. Both take part in athletics, babysit, bag groceries at the supermarket, mow the lawn, prepare meals, and wash the dishes. "That's a boy's job" or "Only girls do that" are comments made less often now than when your parents and your grandparents were your age.

Folks today don't make decisions based only on how things have always been. When they do give thought to what people believed or how people behaved in the past, they will often ask, "But is that right?" Both men and women are employed outside the home today. Women go to the office, travel on business, and support their families financially. Not so long ago these were considered men's tasks. Men spend much more time these days caring for children, doing the marketing, cooking, and cleaning—some of them full time. A few years ago these were things that, in most families, only women did.

Many of the stereotypes are gone. Boys and girls are becoming aware that, first of all, they are persons. The decisions they make about who they are and about what they will become are being made long before the matter of their gender is ever considered. Questions such as *What kind of work is right for a man?* and *What kind of work is right for a woman?* are being replaced by *What do I enjoy doing? What am I good at? What kinds of work would I rather avoid? What things frighten me? What sacrifices am I willing to make in order to reach my goals?* and *What needs are there in the world and how might God be calling me to help meet those needs?*

# CHAPTER 5

# A New Life Begins

The Gift
Friendships With the Other Sex
Commitment
A Celebration of Love
Where Babies Come From
From Embryo to Fetus
A Time to Be Born
Surgical Deliveries
Multiple Births
What Else Might Be On Your Mind?

# The Gift

**Y**ou don't remember it, of course, but several years ago the union of one cell from a male and one cell from a female resulted in something completely new—YOU! "Congratulations! It's a girl" or "It's a boy!" were words that started you on the road to who you are now. Your gender—being female or being male—was a gift to you. The mystery of that gift is something you can spend a lifetime wondering about, exploring, and enjoying.

As you grow and develop, you might think, "Now that I'm going through puberty, I'm becoming a sexual being!" The truth is that you've always been a sexual being. God didn't create us male, female, and put-this-one-on-hold-until-it-

turns-twelve-and-then-we'll-decide. You were destined for maleness or femaleness from the moment those two cells got together—from the moment of your **conception** (kuhn-SEP-shun).

Your body began responding in sexual ways even before you were born. Doctors tell us that even in the womb, males experience erections and females experience vaginal lubrication. These responses are sexual responses—boys responding in certain ways because they are males and girls responding in certain ways because they are females. Such responses do not necessarily mean that a person is thinking about sex or feeling sexy, just that the person is a sexual being, either male or female.

# Friendships With the Other Sex

"**T**he opposite sex" is a phrase you probably hear all the time, but it's one you won't find in this book (except at the beginning of this sentence). Being male does not make me the opposite of a female any more than being female makes someone the opposite of me. Being human gives us so much in common, regardless of our gender, that there's no way for one of us to be the opposite of another. Despite the many differences between males and females, "the other sex" seems to me to be the better way to refer to persons of the gender you're not.

Speaking of the other sex, although for some it happens earlier and for some later, it is usually during the teen years that many boys and girls begin to be interested in persons of the other sex. They find that they like being together—quite a change from just a few years before when boys and girls wanted nothing to do with each other! They begin to date and to enjoy the closeness of holding hands, dancing, hugging, and kissing.

Even more important they begin to tell each other about their hopes, their dreams, and their concerns—stuff that they don't share with just anyone. Remember our discussion of intimacy back in Chapter 4? That's what we've got going on here, and the key part of it is more about talking than touching.

Such young persons are discovering that those who are very different from them can understand their personal thoughts and feelings. While they have been learning about commitment and loyalty through same-sex friendships, they

now see commitment and loyalty from a new perspective—from the perspective of the other sex. They learn to communicate in new ways—through smiles, gentle touches, and being close. These are experiences that prepare young people for lasting relationships.

Adults, as well as older brothers and sisters who think they know everything, sometimes tease us about our first boy-girl relationships. But such friendships are often intense, consuming, and emotional experiences—in part because adolescents tend to experience everything in intense, consuming, and emotional ways.

But these relationships are valuable experiences that help young people grow emotionally and practice responsible decision-making. They help you discover and test out new emotions and help you get to know the special adult person you are in the process of becoming.

# Commitment

In time most people find someone with whom they want to share their lives. They dream and make plans for a life together. They talk about sharing experiences and possessions and, in many cases, plan for the shared experience of parenting. They make a commitment to each other with the understanding that such a commitment will strengthen them individually and strengthen their ability to reach out to others. Good marriages make the world a better place.

*What can I do to make the one I love happy?* is an important concern of husbands and wives. They soon learn that being faithful, honest, and open are some of the keys. They discover the joy of giving and receiving, the joy of exploring all the interesting things about another person. While they respect the ways in which each is different and allow each other the freedom to follow individual interests, they remain committed to the relationship. They laugh together and cry together. They talk to each other about what they are feeling and what they believe. The love they feel at first grows stronger as they meet the challenges of their life together.

# A Celebration of Love

Therefore a man leaves

his father and his mother

and clings to his wife,

and they become one flesh.

Genesis 2:24

When two people love each other and blend their lives in a marriage, they express their love in many ways. A part of most marriages is the joy of sharing bodies in **sexual intercourse**. I say *most* because there are situations—during illness or as a result of physical or emotional limitations—when couples are unable to have sexual intercourse. Such couples discover other ways, through touch and being close, to express tender feelings for each other.

Sexual intercourse is one way in which husbands and wives celebrate their love, friendship, and commitment. Their

**83**

thoughts, words, touches, and kisses prepare them for sexual intercourse. Such actions are referred to as **foreplay** (FOR-play) because they take place before sexual intercourse. These actions or behaviors are sometimes referred to as **pleasuring** in order to emphasize that the pleasure they give to one's partner does not always have to end with intercourse.

In response to these behaviors, the man's penis becomes erect. The women's outer genitals swell, and her vagina becomes moist or lubricated. Should the couple wish to have intercourse, these responses allow the man to insert his penis easily inside the vagina. As their bodies move together, the pleasant feelings become increasingly stronger.

The peak of the man's sexual excitement is orgasm and ejaculation. The woman also can experience an orgasm—the intense and pleasant pulsing of the vaginal walls and of the entire genital area. Some people describe these feelings as being something like a sneeze that builds and builds and finally explodes. Others say that an orgasm is like a wave washing over. Orgasm is the point at which the waves of feeling break over them. Following orgasm the couple relaxes, and both enjoy a sense of contentment.

The frequency of sexual intercourse varies greatly between couples. Couples must decide what feels right for them. The physical expression of love in marriage is celebrated in the Bible in verses such as "Rejoice in the wife of your youth . . . may you be intoxicated always by her love" (from Proverbs 5:18-19), and "My beloved is mine and I am his" (Song of Solomon 2:16a).

# Where Babies Come From

**S**exual intercourse is not just for "making babies," but baby-making is one of the functions it serves. Having a baby can be a very special time—both for the parents-to-be and for others who love them. The decision to have a baby or to engage in behaviors that lead to pregnancy is a big decision that must be made carefully.

In Chapter 2 we described how once every month or so, an ovum is released from one of a female's ovaries into the fallopian tube. If that ovum joins with a sperm following intercourse, conception takes place, and a new life has begun.

Listen once again to these words from Psalm 139 as we begin to explore the creation of a new life.

> For it was you who formed my inward parts;
> you knit me together in my mother's womb.
> I praise you, for I am fearfully
> and wonderfully made.
> Wonderful are your works;
> that I know very well.
> My frame was not hidden from you,
> when I was in being made in secret,
> intricately woven in the depths of the earth.
> Your eyes beheld my unformed substance.
>
> Psalm 139:13-16a

85

The psalm writer imagines God as a weaver, sitting at a loom way in the depths of the earth, weaving together a human form. Ancient peoples knew so little about the origin of human life—even far less than what you know, and yet they were well aware of God's role in this wonder-filled process.

Each time a male ejaculates, millions of tiny sperm are released along with the semen. The semen gives the sperm a major energy boost for the swim ahead. Each sperm is equipped with a tail to propel it from the vagina, through the uterus, and into the fallopian tube. Not all of the sperm will go the distance. Only the strongest will make it all the way to the fallopian tube. The first one to reach the ovum and penetrate the outer shell is responsible for **fertilization** (FER-tuhl-uh-ZAY-shun). Immediately a chemical reaction takes place in that outer shell, and no other sperm can get inside.

At the moment of fertilization when the female and male cells join, many things are determined. In Chapter 3 we mentioned the genes that determine which traits you will inherit from your parents—hair, skin, and eye color; height; when and how quickly you will mature; and so forth. The genes are located on the chromosomes, which are part of every cell in your body.

One of the chromosomes contributed by the ovum is an X chromosome. Sperm, on the other hand, can contain either an X or a Y chromosome. If the ovum is fertilized by a sperm with an X chromosome, the resulting XX combination will direct the development of a female. If the ovum is fertilized by a Y-carrying sperm, the XY combination will direct the development of a male. Lots more has to happen before the female and male organs develop, but the X and Y chromosomes get things moving in that direction.

# Sperm Meets Ovum

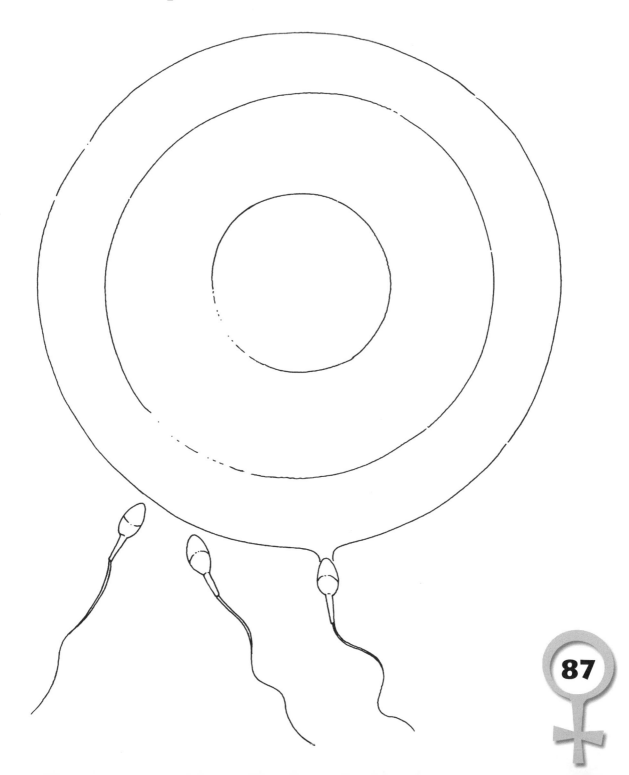

# From Embryo to Fetus

**L**et's get back to the fertilized ovum. The fertilized ovum begins as a single cell and then divides again and again as it moves from the fallopian tube into the uterus. In the uterus it attaches to the nutrient-rich lining. From about the tenth day following conception, this cluster of fast-growing cells is called an **embryo** (EM-bree-oh). After three months the embryo is called a **fetus** (FEE-tuhs).

The specific connection between the embryo and the mother is the **umbilical** (umh-BILL-uh-kuhl) **cord** that forms to link the embryo and the **placenta** (pluh-SEN-tuh). Food and oxygen are received directly from the mother's bloodstream into the placenta, and then through the umbilical cord to the embryo. The elimination of waste takes place in the same way.

Because of this direct linkage, an expectant mother is advised to eat properly and to avoid all drugs unless they are prescribed by her doctor—that includes alcohol, tobacco, and caffeine. Whatever the mother takes into her body, she shares with her growing child. Remember that our bodies are made up of chemicals. The growth of the embryo and fetus is a series of chemical reactions. You can see how the presence of foreign chemicals in the body could affect a child's development—sometimes drastically—and can amount to an act of abuse.

During pregnancy the baby is surrounded and protected by the **amnion** (AM-nee-uhn) or **amniotic** (am-nee-AH-tik) **sac**. The baby is suspended in the watery fluid inside the sac. The amnion also can serve as a warning that the baby is ready to be born.

# Fetal Development

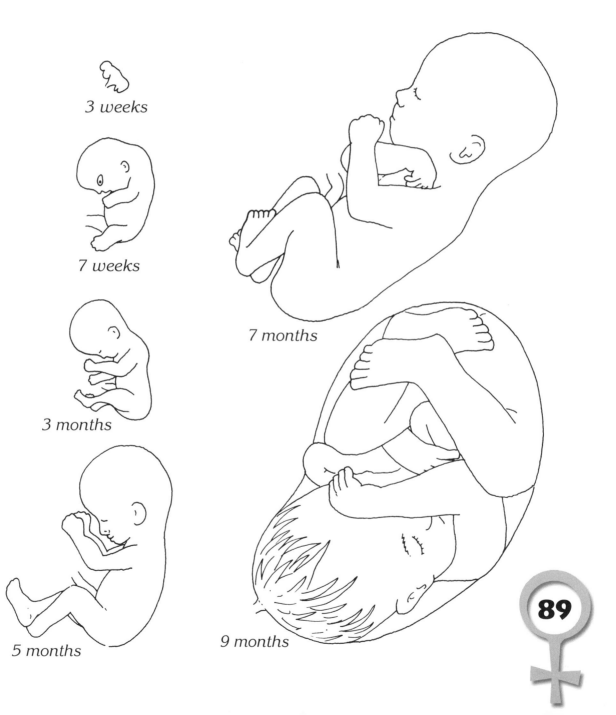

3 weeks

7 weeks

3 months

5 months

7 months

9 months

89

# A Time to Be Born

The length of an average pregnancy is nine months or 40 weeks. At the end of that time the pituitary gland secretes a hormone that causes the birthing process to begin. The muscles of the uterus begin to **contract** (kuhn-TRACT) or shorten. These **contractions** (kuhn-TRACK-shuns) of the uterine muscles are mild and far apart at the beginning of **labor**, which is what we call what is happening as the mother's body moves the baby into position for birth.

As labor continues, the contractions become stronger, come more often, and last longer. They push the baby downward toward the cervix—the lower end of the uterus. The increasing pressure of the baby against the cervix causes the cervix to **dilate** (DIE-late) or open up.

At some point during labor the amniotic sac breaks, and the woman feels a gush or leaking of fluid as it flows from the uterus and out of the vagina. If you have heard people talk about an expectant mother whose water broke, this is what they were talking about. If the sac has not broken on its own during labor, the doctor will break it. Once the cervix has opened enough for the baby to pass through, the baby, usually head first, is pushed through the vagina and out of the body—the step called **delivery**.

Giving birth is hard work for the mother, which explains why the time it takes to position a baby for birth is called labor. It is a time of considerable discomfort. Many couples spend the last several weeks of pregnancy attending childbirth training classes. In these classes the couple is instructed in proper breathing techniques, how to focus attention on

# Stages of Childbirth

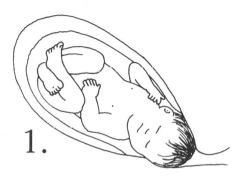

1.

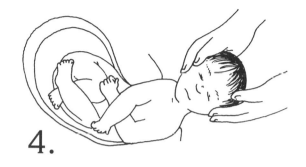

4.

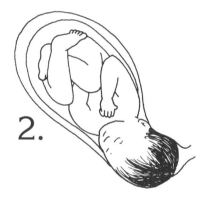

2.

5.

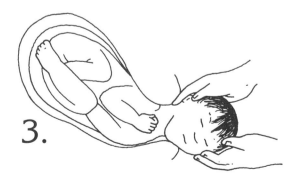

3.

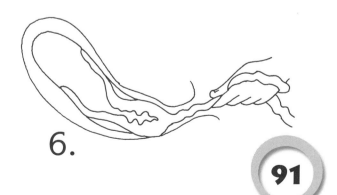

6.

91

something other than the pain, and how the father can coach the mother during labor and delivery. Simply knowing about labor and delivery can help reduce worries and reduce discomfort. Also, there are a variety of medications that can be given to the mother, if needed, to relieve the pain in the latter part of labor and delivery.

Once the baby is born, the umbilical cord is cut and clamped or tied, separating the baby from the mother. No, it doesn't hurt since the umbilical cord doesn't contain nerve tissue. The contractions continue until they push the placenta out of the uterus. For several weeks following the delivery, bleeding may continue as the mother's body rids itself of tissue that was required during pregnancy but is no longer needed.

# Surgical Deliveries

Although most births are vaginal deliveries (babies delivered through the vagina) in the method just described, others are delivered surgically by **caesarean** (sih-ZARE-ee-uhn) **section**. The doctor makes incisions through the abdominal wall (tummy) and the uterus of the mother, and lifts the baby from the uterus. Such deliveries are normal, and babies born by caesarian section can be as healthy as those delivered vaginally, although mothers giving birth by caesarian section may need a longer time to recover than do mothers who deliver vaginally. Julius Caesar is believed to have been delivered surgically, which is how this procedure came to be known as a caesarian section.

A surgical delivery may be performed when the baby is in

a **breech position** (not head first) that would make vaginal delivery dangerous for the baby or the mother. Occasionally a mother has a medical problem that makes vaginal delivery impossible or unsafe. Sometimes caesarian sections are done when a baby has a particularly large head or is experiencing some kind of distress and must be delivered quickly. Multiple births frequently require surgical delivery.

# Multiple Births

Those of us who lead studies on sexuality know that boys and girls generally have lots and lots of questions about multiple births. Do you recall how, following conception, the cells begin to divide? Sometimes these cells split completely apart, and two babies develop instead of one. Why doesn't each develop into just half of a baby? Because both halves contain all the genetic information needed to guide the development

93

of a whole baby. These babies are always the same sex and have identical genetic information because they developed from the same ovum and sperm, so they are called **identical**. If one or more of the cell clusters split again, you could have identical triplets, quadruplets, and so forth.

Sometimes the ovary releases more than one ovum. These ova are then fertilized by different sperm, and two or more embryos develop. These multiple babies are called **fraternal** and since they were fertilized by different sperm, they may or may not be the same sex.

**Conjoined twins** are the result of incomplete cell division. The cluster of cells divide, but a portion remains connected. Two babies develop, but they end up being connected at some part of their bodies and often share one or more organs. These are also known as Siamese twins.

Unusual conceptions such as this often result in a **spontaneous abortion** (spah-TAY-nee-uhs ah-BORE-shuhn) or **miscarriage** (MISS-kare-ihj). The mother's body recognizes that there are serious problems with the embryo or fetus, and automatically ends the pregnancy. Because this experience is much like a menstrual period, women often don't even know what has happened, especially if it takes place early during the pregnancy.

# What Else Might Be on Your Mind?

The subject of pregnancy and babies tends to raise all kinds of questions in young people. Here are a few that girls and boys have asked.

### "How does a woman know when she is pregnant?"

Once pregnancy has occurred, the menstrual periods stop, so not having a period is the first sign that a woman is pregnant. However, since other factors—involvement in athletics, poor health, and emotional stress, for example—can affect the regularity of the menstrual cycle, other special tests must be done to make sure that a woman is pregnant.

Some women experience what is often called **morning sickness**. Particularly during the first three months, women may have an upset stomach in response to their pregnancy. Many who experience this condition do so in the morning, although this is not always the case.

Other changes in the body are signs of pregnancy. The breasts become sensitive to the touch and enlarge, preparing to produce milk for the mother to breastfeed her baby if she chooses to feed her baby in this way. The abdomen enlarges to accommodate the baby growing inside. As the uterus grows, it presses on the bladder, causing pregnant women to need to urinate more often.

Yes, some women do experience cravings for certain foods while they are pregnant. Cravings can be the body's way of asking for certain types of nourishment. The radical changes taking place in a woman's body as the baby grows inside her can account for new dietary demands by her body.

**"Do couples have sexual intercourse during pregnancy?"**

Yes. The fetus is well-protected in the uterus. The amniotic sac is filled with fluid that serves to cushion the baby inside. Unless there is a problem with the pregnancy where the mother must be unusually careful, most couples can continue having sexual intercourse until close to the time of birth—or until it becomes too uncomfortable to do so.

**"I guess I knew that my parents had sexual intercourse. After all, they had me! But I never thought that they did it regularly!"**

Few parents talk freely with their children about this part of their marriage. Sexual intercourse is a private thing that husbands and wives enjoy together. At the same time children need to know that this is a part of their parents' relationship. Sometimes girls and boys interpret their parents' silence as evidence that their mothers and fathers are not sexually active. So when they begin to have sexual feelings about someone and need to make some important decisions, they assume that their parents won't understand.

Many children (maybe you) have had the experience of rushing in unannounced to their parents' bedroom and finding Mom and Dad in a moment of sexual closeness. Beyond the embarrassment there is something to be learned. Parents do enjoy the physical part of being in love, and they need private times to express their love in a way that God fully intended for them. They have had and continue to have those feelings too.

## "What is a virgin?"

In biblical times the word **virgin** meant a young woman but also was used to refer to a woman who had not yet had sexual intercourse. The same word now applies to both females and males.

An unstretched or untorn hymen was once believed to be proof that a girl was still a virgin. Tradition said that a true virgin would bleed when the hymen was penetrated by the penis during the first experience of sexual intercourse. As was mentioned in Chapter 2 many factors can account for the absence of the hymen. The presence or absence of the hymen is not proof of a female's virginity.

## "Does it hurt to have sexual intercourse?"

Generally, no. I say *generally* because that answer needs a couple of explanations. The first is this: Since the vagina of a female who has not had sexual intercourse has not been stretched, she may experience some discomfort the first time or two that she has intercourse. The second is connected to the differences between how men and women respond to sexual stimulation.

Men respond more quickly and thus tend to be ready for sexual intercourse before their partners are ready. Women respond more gradually and are stimulated by loving words and touches. If intercourse is attempted before a woman is ready physically and emotionally, it can be uncomfortable for both persons. A loving man will be sensitive to his partner's needs and not try to rush into something for which his partner is not ready.

### "When are people finished being sexual?"

Never. Being sexual is part of what it means to be human. Since we are human at the moment of our conception and continue to be human throughout life, we are sexual all of that time as well.

Our society is paying more attention and being more sensitive to the sexuality of people who we once treated as nonsexual. You, for example. Girls and boys are sexual beings with sexual thoughts and sexual feelings. Another example is older adults who continue to need intimacy and physical closeness long after they have ceased to fit the stereotypes for sexy women or men—long after women have stopped menstruating, which is called **menopause** (MEHN-uh-pahz). The same is true with people who have physical or mental disabilities. To be created in the image of God is to be created male or female. All persons are sexual always.

### Who's going to answer the rest of my questions?

If you are anything like the hundreds of young people (and parents) I've worked with in human sexuality studies over the past several years, you have a zillion questions about your body, about other bodies, about babies, and about relationships. Each of your questions is important and deserves an answer. I trust that you're finding answers to lots of those questions in this book, but you will no doubt have questions we either didn't think of or didn't have space to cover.

Amazingly enough, parents and other adults can be a good source of answers. Some adults are uncomfortable with questions about bodies and sexuality and will put off giving answers, saying, "Let's discuss this later." Some pretend not to hear the questions. While making adults uncomfortable seldom pays off, with a little patience you might find a better time to ask your questions, or a better way of asking them. Don't give up. Your questions are an opportunity for everyone—young people and adults—to learn and to grow.

Begin with family members. Your parents, grandparents, aunts, uncles, older sisters, brothers, and cousins have had the same questions and concerns that you are having now. Really! They might need to be reminded that they were once your age, since people sometimes forget.

Many things have changed since your parents and grandparents were experiencing adolescence. That's important for you and for them to remember. If you have brothers or sisters who are considerably older than you, some things will have changed since the time they were your age. More information is available. People ask their questions differently and look at life differently.

Look to other responsible adults—a teacher, pastor, Sunday school teacher, friend's parent, coach, pediatrician or family doctor, school counselor, scout leaders, or next-door neighbor. Maybe they'll have answers to your questions, and maybe they won't. If they don't, they'll probably be willing to give you a hand at finding the information you need. There are times when it's easier to talk with someone who is not a parent—or at least not your parent. We are afraid that we will worry or upset our parents by asking some questions. But we still need answers. Go get them!

Many young persons and parents are finding that the best way to get answers to questions, or just to get conversations started, is to take part in a group study of human sexuality. Group studies give everyone basic information, offer a chance to practice using proper terms, and allow everyone to ask his or her particular questions. My experience is that lots of young people are hesitant to commit the time to such a study, but

afterward are glad they did. Schools and hospitals offer studies, but my experience is that the church does the best job when it comes to human sexuality education. When we ask the big questions, it's important not to leave God out of the answers!

Finally, read! Books can be good sources of accurate information. Start out by finishing this book. Between here and the last page you ought to run across the answers to a few more of your questions. Then visit your public library or the library at your school or church. Check out a local bookstore. When you have questions about what's going on inside and outside your body—read, read, read! Study the diagrams and read what the writer has to say. As you read, you'll probably come up with new questions to ask.

Your sexuality is a wonderful gift from God! You'll have many decisions to make in the years ahead as to what you'll do with this wonderful gift. The many questions you have now and will have in the future will help you make those decisions. Ask those questions, and keep asking until you get the answers you need!

# CHAPTER 6

# A Look Inside the Question Box

The Lid Comes Off
Language
Masturbation
Friends of the Same Gender
Dating and Boy-Girl Relationships
Abstinence
Homosexuality
Family Planning
Abortion
Sex and Advertising
Prostitution
Sexual Abuse
STDs and AIDS
Pornography
Being Response-Able

101

# The Lid Comes Off

**A**dolescence means increasing opportunities to be on your own and to make your own decisions. In this chapter we'll discuss matters about which you will have decisions to make. Our discussion will be frank because these matters can affect your well-being and are things that confuse, concern, and even frighten young persons.

No, this final chapter isn't all gloom and doom. When Paul wrote to Christians in Philippi, he knew they were dealing with their own set of confusing stuff. In one of my favorite Scripture verses, he wrote, "Finally, beloved, whatever is true, whatever is honorable, whatever is just, whatever is pure, whatever is pleasing, whatever is commendable, if there is any excellence and if there is anything worthy of praise, think about these things" (Philippians 4:8). Paul wisely knew that in order to make room for all of these positive thoughts, we need to clear out negatives such as confusion, ignorance, and worry.

Like Chapter 5, this last chapter responds to questions boys and girls raise during human sexuality studies taking place in churches all over the country. Sometimes they come right out and ask their questions and get answers on the spot. Sometimes they write them down on a card and place them anonymously in the Question Box for the leaders to respond to at the appropriate time.

You've probably heard of Pandora's box. According to Greek mythology Pandora was the first woman, and she was entrusted with a box that contained all the bad things that could happen to humankind. Her curiosity led her to open the box. The myth says that all that evil went flying everywhere, which explains its presence in the world.

103

As I sit with young people, listening to all of their questions or reading questions they have written and placed in the question box, I sometimes feel like it's Pandora's box I'm opening—although it's honest wondering rather than evil that comes flying out. You have so many questions to ask, and because of all the decisions ahead of you, you're looking for answers. As young persons of faith you need accurate information in order to be responsible decision-makers. So let's open up the question box and let some information fly.

# Language

**Why do you use scientific names instead of the other words (the easier words)?**

That question is word-for-word right out of the question box. It was asked by a young person who was feeling overwhelmed with all of the terms that had been introduced during the sexuality education event. I can understand the feeling, but still encouraged the group to practice the proper terms.

Throughout this book we've given you lots of words, but we haven't said much about language in general. Girls and boys want to know what kind of language to use when they talk about their bodies and about their sexuality. They also wonder about the sexual jokes they hear.

When I lead studies for young persons and their parents, I review some of the slang terms that we hear used in reference to bodies and behaviors. They think it's strange or funny to hear these "bad" or "dirty" terms spoken out loud by an

adult—especially by a pastor. I guess if I were in their shoes, I'd think the same thing.

I don't share these slang terms to shock anyone or to encourage their use. My goal is to pass along information that helps girls and boys understand what they are hearing and learn to translate what they are hearing into proper terminology.

When it comes to language, the words themselves aren't what is good or bad, but how those words are used. Words can be used to hurt, and words can be used to help. Words can be used to make persons feel good about themselves or to make them feel bad about themselves. For example, most of the slang terms that refer to sexual intercourse also are used to refer to hurtful and even violent actions. Is that the understanding of intercourse that we want to communicate to others?

Words scribbled on the walls of a public bathroom or sprayed on the side of a building aren't generally ones we are comfortable using around parents or other adults. It isn't that they wouldn't know these words. Chances are they would. Street language hasn't changed that much over the years. Its object is to get a reaction. Language has that kind of power. Certain words can cause embarrassment and anger. Some persons like to have the power to embarrass and to anger others.

You probably know persons who are only able to talk about sexuality when they are joking about it. They usually can find an audience for their jokes, so they get lots of practice and become comfortable with the jokes and slang terms. They are uncomfortable using the correct words because they don't have a chance to practice using those words. I would encourage you to practice the proper terms until you become comfortable with them. The best words are the ones that communicate most clearly.

105

# Masturbation

What is masturbation?

What happens if
someone masturbates
too much?

From the time you were born, you learned by experiencing the world around you. You looked, listened, smelled, tasted, and touched. You have been curious about your body since you were a baby, learning to point to and name your ears, nose, eyes, mouth, hands, feet, and other body parts. You investigated what each one did.

The investigation continues today because your curiosity continues. You test yourself to see how long you can hold your breath, how much weight you can lift, how high you can reach, or how fast you can run. You experiment in order to know what it feels like to walk barefoot over hot pavement, through a freezing stream, or across a muddy path.

Curiosity has led you to some important discoveries about yourself. Exploring the feel of your body as a little child, you became aware of and discovered its various parts—including your genitals. As a result of such exploration, children discover that touching the genitals causes pleasant sensations.

Girls and boys also find that this activity sometimes evokes rather strong responses from adults. Some adults attempt to halt the activity in young children with a firm, "Stop that!" Others hurriedly try to distract the child. In such cases children quickly learn that these activities do not meet with adults' approval. The confusion that results is understandable! Why is it, children might wonder, that such nice feelings come from actions that are considered wrong? This might be a question you're asking yourself right now.

The Bible's silence on the topic of masturbation suggests that it is not a moral problem. The troublesome thing about masturbation is the worry it causes. People worry that they will be caught; worry that others will somehow know that they have been masturbating; worry that they might harm themselves; worry that God will disapprove of them. Note that although Jesus didn't have anything to say about masturbation, he clearly understood worry to be a waste of time. "And can any of you by worrying add a single hour to your span of life?" (Matthew 6:27).

While rough handling of the genitals could cause temporary irritation and soreness, masturbation is unlikely to damage the sex organs. Males will not "run out" of semen or sperm if they masturbate. Their bodies will continue to produce more. Females will not lessen their ability to become pregnant. Masturbation does not physically affect one's ability to enjoy sexual relations as an adult.

As you think about all of the opportunities, challenges, and fun that are available in the world God has created for us, you may conclude (along with Jesus) that doing things that cause us to worry doesn't make much sense. For many people masturbation fits into this category.

Masturbation is a private activity. Most persons engage in this private activity at some time during their lives, and many continue to do so throughout their lives. What is "too much" when it comes to masturbation? That's hard to say. Having

talked with lots of folks about masturbation, researchers find that more males masturbate and masturbate more often than females. Some persons masturbate several times a day; some, every day or so; some, just once in a while; and some never masturbate at all. No one can say what is right or normal for everyone.

In spite of masturbation being a very natural experience, the worry often remains. If it should become a worrisome thing for you, remember that the problem is worry, not masturbation.

At the same time, anything we do that takes too much of our energy or prevents us from spending time with other people needs to be questioned. You want to be doing things that make you feel good about yourself. Feeling good about yourself, as we talked about in Chapter 4, helps you to love others and to love God. If masturbation seems to prevent you from feeling good about yourself, find someone to talk with—a friend, a parent, or another adult you trust. Believe me, it won't be difficult to find someone who understands from personal experience what you are going through. Sometimes just talking with an understanding person helps relieve the worry.

# Friends of the Same Gender

At what age should you start liking girls?

At what age should you start liking boys?

The years of childhood and adolescence are some of the most exciting. With so much change happening, it's hard to know what to expect next. Put two changing people together, and you more than double the excitement! But because of all the change, friendships are not always easy during these years. They are important, and they are often very strong, but they're not easy.

Right now your best friends are probably girls if you are a girl, and boys if you are a boy. These tend to be the persons with whom you have spent the most time and have the most in common. Girls and boys are sometimes concerned about these friendships when they hear about persons who are **homosexual**—sexually attracted to or sexually active with persons of their own sex.

It is not unusual for sexual contact between boys and between girls to take place after the innocent playing house or playing doctor that goes on between children. Again, this is, for some young people, a way of investigating the new bodies

109

and new feelings that have come with adolescence. Having special feelings for a same-sex friend is typical at your age.

Something else that is very common at your age is the boy who has strong feelings for a man—a teacher, coach, or camp counselor, for example. Girls your age often have strong feelings for women in similar positions. As you think about who you are becoming, you see qualities in others that you admire—qualities related to appearance or personality that you hope others will someday see in you. It is natural to be attracted to people we admire. You have not invented something new!

Try making a list of the things you admire in such a person, and choose from that list those qualities you'd like to set as goals for yourself. As you pray, thank God for the presence of persons whom you want to be like. Ask God to help you reach these goals and to find just the right person with whom you can share these thoughts and feelings.

# Dating and Boy-Girl Relationships

What do people do on a date?

What's the right age to begin dating?

How can you tell when someone likes you?

Why are boys so weird?

Why are girls so weird?

How do you know when you're in love?

**T**hese are all real questions asked by real girls and boys your age. Dating is not something many people your age are doing, although some are. In any case it's natural for you to be wondering what happens on a date.

Dating is one way young people get to know each other. In many ways dating is like any other act of friendship. You talk, laugh, do things, and go places together. Friendships generally start with things that people have in common: living near each other, liking the same kind of music, playing on the same team, sitting beside each other in class—those sorts of things. Friends who are dating have things in common too, but the fact that they are not of the same sex adds a new and

special element. People are drawn together not just because they are alike in many ways, but also because they are different. The differences give them lots to talk and learn about!

First-time daters are usually nervous. They have to think through some new questions: *How do I order if we go out to eat? Do we pay for our own meals or movie tickets, or does the boy always pay for both? Should we be holding hands? What about kissing—who starts and when is it okay? Eyes open or shut? How late can we be out?*

Here it comes again! Dating can be fun—especially when people talk to each other. Be honest. Tell your date how nervous you feel. Chances are your date feels the same way. Decide ahead of time who's going to pay for the meal or the movie. Why not share the expenses? Better yet, why not do "group dating" for a while? Having two or more couples together seems to be more comfortable for everyone—more persons, more experiences, more to talk about.

Dating can present problems when respect for self and others isn't given a high priority. Be smart. Understand yourself, your feelings, and the way your mind and body react when you are close to another person, holding hands, hugging, and kissing. Talking together about these matters shows your care and respect for each other.

The "weirdness" boys see in girls and girls see in boys has to do with a lack of experience being with one another. I suppose it's human nature to classify someone different from us as being weird, but God certainly calls us to grow in our acceptance of those who are different. Spending time

getting to know one another is the only solution I can offer for the weirdness.

Let's suppose that you've moved beyond the "weird" question—far enough to recognize special feelings for a particular person and to wonder if you're falling in love. You've observed people who appear to be or claim to be in love. You see people who once were in love but aren't anymore. Were they really in love? Were they mistaken? Did they fall out of love? The lives of many girls and boys have been touched directly by the divorce of parents or indirectly by the divorce of other family members, neighbors, or friends' parents. Are there ways to avoid making mistakes?

We start by realizing that we were created by God to love many people, not just one. There are many people who are possible lifelong partners for us, not just one. You will be meeting lots of people in the next several years. You will be developing friendships with some of those people. With some of those friends you will work at building intimacy. Perhaps there will be one special person you will decide to marry— one person to whom you will commit your life.

The question *How will I know when I'm in love?* tends to be more a question of feeling than of knowing. We expect that our bodies are going to give us some very specific signals. It's true that our bodies do respond in certain ways when we are attracted to another person. But the responses of our bodies don't always tell us who we should or shouldn't consider as marriage partners.

Let me give you some other questions to ask yourself: *Who do I enjoy being with more than anyone else? Who makes me feel good about myself? Who do I always enjoy discovering new things about? Who values the things I consider to be important? Who wants to be close to me but doesn't insist that we do everything together? Who do I trust with my personal thoughts and feelings?*

113

In some marriage services, the pastor concludes the ceremony with these words to the couple:

God the Eternal keep you in love with each other,
so that the peace of Christ may abide in your home.
Go to serve God and your neighbor in all that you do.

Then the pastor says to everyone:

Bear witness to the love of God in this world,
so that those to whom love is a stranger
will find in you generous friends.

From "A Service of Christian Marriage" in *The United Methodist Hymnal*; © 1989
The United Methodist Publishing House; p. 869. Reprinted by permission.

What you feel for and experience with one person sometimes brings out the very best in you and helps you to be more loving toward others. This may be a good sign that you are in love.

# Abstinence

"Why should I wait until I'm married to have sexual intercourse?"

It's true that from early adolescence young people are physically capable of sexual intercourse. Girls and boys become sexually excited. Unfortunately some allow themselves to get into situations where sexual intercourse can and does happen.

Remember the word *intimacy* we talked about in Chapter 4? As we said back then, intimacy is much more than a closeness of bodies. Intimacy is a closeness of whole persons. Intimacy is two persons really knowing each other. Intimacy is loving another person just as he or she is. For many persons sexual intercourse becomes a part of intimacy. But sexual intercourse and intimacy are not the same thing. Intimacy takes time. Intimacy requires honesty, and honesty is pretty difficult for two young persons feeling guilty because they have become involved in sexual intercourse.

Why wait to have sexual intercourse? Here are five reasons that I think (and I hope you agree) make sense:

**1.** Young persons who have sexual intercourse end up missing out on all of the talking that leads to intimacy. Guilt and embarrassment prevent them from talking with each other about sex or anything else. Sexual intercourse is a good gift, but when this good gift is used unwisely, it can destroy intimacy.

As Paul writes to the people of the Corinthian church, "Love is patient" (1 Corinthians 13:4a). Being patient when it comes to sexual intercourse is an act of kindness—toward yourself, toward that person for whom you have special feelings, and toward the many other people who stand to be affected if you make the decision to have sexual relations while you are young.

Setting yourself up to feel guilty is foolish. Not thinking of the many people who will be affected by your actions is selfish. It is not unusual for young persons to have little upon which to build a lasting relationship, but they feel forced to stay together because they have had or are having intercourse.

**2.** Pregnancy can happen. The first experience of sexual intercourse can result in pregnancy. Many young persons who

115

become sexually active do not practice any form of birth control. (See the section in this chapter called "Family Planning.") Even if they do, they need to realize that no form of birth control other than **abstinence** (AB-stuh-nuhns) or not having intercourse is 100 percent effective. Persons who choose to have intercourse should be prepared for the possibility of pregnancy and all of its responsibilities.

**3.** Along the same lines the younger the mother, the greater the likelihood that there will be complications during pregnancy and delivery. Young girls' bodies are not fully prepared for motherhood. Babies born to teenaged mothers are often underweight and are frequently born prematurely (weeks or even months before the end of a normal nine-month pregnancy). The death rate for premature babies born to teenaged mothers is higher than the death rate for premature babies in general. Teenaged mothers are more likely not to receive proper **prenatal** (pree-NAY-tuhl) **care**—medical care for mothers and babies during pregnancy. This also adds to the risks.

**4.** Young persons are not emotionally prepared for parenthood. Parenting is hard work for parents of all ages, but even more so for young people who still have lots of physical and emotional growth ahead of them. In a majority of situations a baby puts more pressure on young parents than their relationship can take.

**5.** Young persons are not financially prepared for parenthood. Parenting is not only difficult, but it is also expensive. Teenaged parents often drop out of school. Their lack of education makes it difficult to get good jobs. In many cases teenagers who become parents face a lifetime of financial struggles.

Perhaps you've read or heard how important it is for babies to crawl before they walk. Something is happening during the crawling stage that helps develop the coordination between a little person's eyes and hands. Important stuff is happening during that period when one is waiting to walk. Children who walk before they crawl or who spend too little time crawling may have coordination-related difficulties later on.

So it is with sexual intercourse. Some young people believe that having a child will make them instant adults. Although becoming a teenaged parent pushes young people into adult responsibilities, it can't provide them with the adult maturity that is needed to handle those responsibilities. Teenagers who become parents cheat themselves out of the time they need to grow into adulthood naturally. Young people are wise to wait.

While this statement is obvious, it needs to be said: Young people can avoid these problems with the decision not to be sexually active. We believe, as Christian people, that abstinence is a decision that reflects the will of God for the lives of young people. It is a difficult decision to make, and often even more difficult to keep. Many girls and boys find that having friends who have also made a commitment to abstinence, with whom they can talk about it, and lend support in moments of temptation, can be helpful. The writer of Ecclesiastes helps with the reminder that for everything there is a season, including "a time to embrace, and a time to refrain from embracing" (3:5). The "embrace" the writer speaks of is making love. For young bodies, minds, and lives, the time is not yet right.

# Homosexuality

What does "homosexual" mean?

Why are some people homosexuals?

**P**ersons who are **heterosexual** (HEHT-uh-roh-SEHK-shoo-uhl) are sexually attracted to or sexually active with persons of the other sex. Persons who are homosexual are sexually attracted to or sexually active with persons of the same sex. Both male and female homosexuals are sometimes referred to as being **gay**, although this word is mostly used in reference to male homosexuals. Female homosexuals are sometimes referred to as **lesbians** (LEZ-bee-uhnz). *Gay* and *lesbian* are words many homosexual persons use to speak of their sexuality. A **bisexual** (bie-SEKS-yoo-uhl) person is one who is sexually attracted to or sexually active with persons of both sexes. This attraction is called one's **sexual orientation** (or-ee-en-TAY-shun). While these three sexual orientations may appear to be very distinct or separate, in reality the divisions are not so clear. Every individual is different.

Why are some people homosexuals? Much research has been done on the subject by doctors, psychologists, educators, and theologians; but they have yet to agree on a reason. There are most likely many factors that determine to whom one is attracted. So the honest answer to the question is this: We do not know.

Remember that this orientation is only one factor in what makes a person who he or she is. People are just people. Some of them fit cultural stereotypes for femininity or masculinity, and some of them don't. That goes for all people. Observing a person's interest, behaviors, or body type cannot tell us what that person's sexual orientation might be.

Not having clear-cut answers we tend to feel confused and even afraid—feelings that sometimes cause us to be less than loving. Learning about things—and people—that frighten and confuse us can take away the fear and confusion.

Instead of basing our actions on what we don't know—such as why people represent a variety of sexual orientations—we need to act on what we do know. We know that we are created by God and loved by God. We know that, as children of God, we must never hurt others by taking advantage of their sexual feelings or of what they do or do not know or understand about their sexuality. These things apply to all of us, regardless of our sexual orientation.

Remember Jesus' story of the Good Samaritan? A man was beaten by robbers and left to die. Two persons passed by. The first was a priest. The second was a Levite—a temple official. They weren't responsible for the problems of the man on the road, but just like the robbers, they also left him to die. It was a Samaritan—a person whom Jesus' listeners wouldn't have had anything to do with—who stopped and cared. Jesus used this story to explain the meaning of "neighbor." The neighbors we are called to love as we love ourselves are often people who are different from us (Luke 10:25-37).

119

# Family Planning

What does "abstinence" mean?

How does a condom work?

**S**ome couples choose not to have children or to limit the size of their families. Having made these choices, they have others to make. When they have sexual intercourse, they must decide about a method of **birth control**. Birth control refers to any method used to prevent pregnancy. Abstinence, which we've already referred to, means abstaining from sexual intercourse or simply not having intercourse. It remains the only 100 percent effective method and is the absolutely wisest and most Godly choice for unmarried persons, but let's briefly review some birth control methods currently in use.

**Natural Family Planning** requires a couple to watch for signs of ovulation—such as the woman's body temperature—and avoid sexual intercourse on days when conception is possible.

The **birth control pill** is taken by the woman at the same time every day. It contains hormones that cause a woman's body to act as though it is pregnant, preventing the release of ova from the ovaries.

The **intrauterine** (in-tra-YOO-truh-in) **device** or **IUD** is a soft plastic or metal ring, coil, or loop that must be inserted into and removed from the uterus by a doctor. Many doctors have questioned the safety of the IUD and hesitate to recommend it as a birth control method.

A **condom** (KON-duhm) looks like a large, rolled-up balloon. It is unrolled over the erect penis of the husband. The condom holds the semen, preventing the sperm from reaching and fertilizing an ovum.

A **diaphragm** (DIE-uh-fram) is a kind of rubber cap, inserted into the vagina by the women before having sexual intercourse. The diaphragm is used along with a **spermicide** (SPER-mih-side). The diaphragm prevents sperm from entering the uterus, and the spermicidal foam destroys the sperm. Spermicides also can be used alone and are inserted deep in the vagina. Spermicides and condoms are more effective when used at the same time.

Two of the newer chemical birth control methods work like the birth control pill, but are easier to use, last longer, and are slightly more effective. The **implant** is six flexible tubes that are implanted under the skin in the upper arm of the woman. Women also can receive birth control by **injection** once every three months.

For couples who choose not to have children or not to have any more children, **sterilization**, which is the surgical process of making a person permanently incapable of reproduction, is available. A **tubal ligation** (TOO-buhl lie-GAY-shun) is an operation where the woman's fallopian tubes are cut, tied, or sealed to prevent pregnancy from occurring. A **vasectomy** (vah-SEHK-tuh-me) is an operation performed on the man that cuts the vas deferens and prevents sperm from mixing with the semen. The ovaries continue to release ova, and the testicles continue to produce sperm, but both ova and sperm are absorbed by the body.

# Abortion

What happens when a person has an abortion?

An **abortion** (uh-BORE-shun) is a medical procedure that terminates or ends a pregnancy. The lining of the uterus and the embryo or fetus are drawn out of the uterus using a suction process. Abortion has been considered when pregnancy has threatened the life of the mother; when tests show that a fetus is seriously deformed; and when the pregnancy is the result of rape (forced sexual intercourse).

Unfortunately many people also see abortion as a means of birth control, using it to end a pregnancy. Teenaged girls who become pregnant often opt for abortion rather than raising the baby or putting it up for adoption. Couples who are not married sometimes make the same decision, as do married parents who for some reason feel unable to add to their family.

The decision to terminate a pregnancy brings an end to a life and must be made with prayer and very careful thought. Some who choose abortion feel deep regret later on. Those faced with this decision need loving support. They need to explore their feelings and to consider how this decision is going to affect them now and later on. Parents, pastors, physicians, friends, and the father of the unborn child are important persons to involve as the decision is made.

Some teenaged mothers place their babies up for adoption—another decision that requires a great deal of support. Enabling a childless couple to have a family and giving a child a better chance in life is a caring thing to do. Giving up a child is a very difficult thing to do and, as with abortion, is something that some parents later regret.

# Sex and Advertising

Why does my mom get so steamed over jeans commercials on TV?

**M**om is steamed because people are using sex and using you to make money. Producing television shows, radio programs, movies, newspapers, and magazines costs money. Some of the money comes from the advertisers—jeans manufacturers and others—who pay to have their products promoted. Some of the money comes from the consumers—the people who go to the movies, read the magazines, and buy the jeans and other products.

our product will make you beautiful!

Think back once again to our discussion of stereotypes in Chapter 3. People who are trying to sell their products create a stereotype—a picture of the ideal girl or boy. By convincing young persons that seeing a movie or buying a product will help make them this ideal girl or boy, advertisers stand to make a lot of money. Being sexually attractive is part of that ideal. How you feel about being a female or male is not the

123

advertisers' concern. Their goal is to create the ideal, then to convince you that you can reach that ideal with their help.

Advertisers also realize how much you want to grow up. They are suggesting to you that you don't have to go through the long maturing process. If you use their product, you can be an adult right now! They're lying to you. No one cuts corners on the way to being all grown up. No one can sell you anything to make the growing faster.

# Prostitution

Why would someone become a prostitute?

A **prostitute** (PROSS-tuh-toot) is a person—a woman, man, girl, or boy—paid to perform sexual acts. Persons who become prostitutes often have convinced themselves that there is no other way for them to earn the money that they need. Persons who set themselves up to be used by others— even when being paid for it—cannot feel good about themselves. Some prostitutes are looking for affection and love, but they are looking in the wrong places.

Prostitutes are frequently the victims of violence. Persons who pay to use a prostitute's body seldom care what happens to the prostitute.

In many cities local newspapers print the names of persons who have been arrested for trying to buy the services of prostitutes. In addition to the legal consequences, these persons often find their lives ruined by the publicity that their actions receive.

Being sexually active with many people puts prostitutes at great risk for being infected with **sexually transmitted diseases (STDs)**. Prostitution is illegal in most places, and it is frequently associated with violence and drug use.

# Sexual Abuse

My babysitter touched me once. What should I do?

What does "rapist" mean?

**F**irst of all, this young person needs to know that he or she did nothing wrong, although others who have had similar experiences often wonder if they have. They wonder what they have done to encourage such people. In most cases their only mistake was being in the wrong place at the wrong time.

Much attention has been given recently to the subject of **sexual abuse**. Here's how I have been explaining sexual abuse to the young persons and parents I work with:

If you are not done growing up
physically, mentally, or emotionally,
and are drawn into sexual activities
you don't completely understand—
because you're not done growing up—
activities that break family rules
or rules followed by our society as a whole
(such as being asked to touch another person's private parts
with your hands, mouth, or your private parts;
having another person touch your private parts;
being asked to look at pornographic pictures;
being asked to pose for pornographic pictures
undressed or engaged in sexual activity);
when you have trouble saying "yes" or "no"
because you don't understand
what you are being encouraged to do
or feel that you are being forced into these activities,
that's called the sexual abuse of a child.
It is always wrong
and it is never your fault.
Tell someone.

The problem of sexual abuse is widespread. We have been telling girls and boys not to talk to strangers or not to get into a car with someone they don't know, but we didn't tell them why. So they wondered. We're doing a better job today. With boys and girls being more aware, hopefully the problem of sexual abuse will decrease.

Who are sex abusers? Sometimes they are strangers, but in most cases they are acquaintances—even friends and relatives. Most sex abusers are men, but women can be abusive as well. Because it is against the law to abuse a person sexually, sex abusers are persons who are guilty of a sexual crime.

Why do they abuse? It has to do, at least in part, with their confusion about sexuality. To abuse something is to use it in an improper or destructive way. That is what sex abusers do with sex. Many were abused as children, leaving them confused about the place of sex in their lives.

The sexual abuse of a child is called **child molesting** (muh-LEST-ing). Forced sexual intercourse is called **rape**. Both girls and boys can be the victims of a **rapist** (RAY-pist)—a male who forces his penis into the vagina, anus, or mouth of his victim; or a female who forces someone to perform a sexual act with her. **Date rape** is when a female is forced against her will to have sex with someone she is dating.

When the abuser and the victim are members of the same family, it is called **incest** (IN-sest). Incest is hard to understand. The victim wants the abuse to stop but is afraid of losing the love of the abuser. The victim also might worry about what will happen to the family if the abuse is reported. Sometimes abusive family members will use the possible breakup of the family as a threat to keep the victim quiet.

Some sex abusers give their victims alcohol or drugs in order to make them cooperate. Some will try to convince their victims that such acts are normal, that everyone is sexually active, or that the act is something that the victim really wants. Some say that performing such acts is a sign that a person is growing up or is an expression of love. Some will

even try to get a victim to believe that he or she deserves the abuse because of something the victim did in the past. If someone tries to convince you with a statement like these, don't believe it!

Some sex abusers physically overpower their victims. Some threaten to harm their victims or their victim's friends, family, pets, or home if they don't cooperate. Sex abusers often threaten the same harm if the victim tells anyone what has happened.

Once again, sexual abuse in any form is always wrong, and it is never the fault of the victim. Should that victim be you or someone you know, tell someone. If the first person doesn't listen or respond, tell someone else, and keep telling until someone does listen. Nobody deserves to be abused.

Victims of abuse frequently need medical attention. Girls who have begun menstruating and who are rape victims need immediate medical care in order to ensure that pregnancy does not occur. The victims of any kind of sexual abuse need the support of persons who can help the victims through this frightening experience. When sexual abuse happens within families, everyone in the family will need help in understanding and getting over the abuse. The threats of abusers should be ignored. We have laws to protect the victims of abuse.

You don't have to worry every minute about being abused, but it's smart to be cautious. Avoid being alone in places where it would be difficult to get help if you needed it. Don't assume that all strangers are sex abusers, but be careful. Learn to listen carefully to what people are saying to you. The many excuses that persons give to convince young people to become sexually involved don't make sense.

Learn to listen to your body. Your body will often tell you that it's afraid before your mouth is able to say so. Trust your feelings. Understand your body and your sexuality. This understanding will help you to be aware of possible abuse and to do something about it. Talk with others. A team effort can make you even safer.

# STDs and AIDS

What's an STD?

Can you get AIDS from just kissing?

Could you get HIV from tattoos?

Before you have sexual intercourse, can you get tested for HIV?

**S**exually transmitted diseases (STDs) are infectious diseases passed from one person to another through sexual contact. There are more than twenty different STDs. The seven major STDs are **syphilis** (SIF-uh-luhs), **gonorrhea** (gahn-uh-REE-uh), **chlamydia** (KLUH-mid-ee-uh), **genital herpes** (HER-peez), **genital warts**, **hepatitis B** (HEP-uh-TIE-tihs), and **acquired immune deficiency syndrome** (uh-KWIRED ih-MUNE duh-FISH-uhn-see SIN-drohm) or **AIDS**.

129

Some STDs can be treated and cured; others can't. Persons who have an incurable STD will have this disease for life and will continue to be able to pass it to others.

The following symptoms are sometimes associated with STDs:

Unusual discharges (leaking of a thick fluid) from the penis or vagina

Unusual odor from the genital area

Itching or burning in the genital area

A rash or sore in the genital area, anal area, or mouth

Abdominal pain or tenderness

Pain or burning during urination

Fatigue

Night sweats

These symptoms do not automatically mean that a person has an STD. In fact a person can have an STD and have no symptoms at all. These symptoms also can indicate the presence of other diseases—diseases that are not sexually transmitted. However, persons who are sexually active and have any of these symptoms are advised to see their doctor.

STD germs need the proper conditions to survive—conditions found in places such as the penis, vulva, vagina, rectum, mouth, or throat. In order to pass the germ from one body to another, there must be direct contact of "STD survival places" between two persons. This kind of contact generally happens during sexual activity.

Most STD germs die soon after they leave the body and are exposed to the air. This fact makes it unusual for STDs to spread in ways other than human-to-human contact. Certain STD germs can be passed from an expectant mother to her unborn child and can cause a variety of birth defects in the child.

The **Human Immunodeficiency** (ih-MYOO-noh-duh-FIH-shuhn-see) **Virus** or **HIV** attacks the body's immune system—the system that fights off disease. AIDS is the result. The body is unable to defend itself against diseases that it normally could fight off—pneumonia, for example—and some rare diseases that people with healthy immune systems seldom get. The first cases of AIDS in the United States were recorded in 1981. Since then thousands of deaths throughout the world have resulted from AIDS-related complications.

Having sexual relations with someone infected with HIV is the most common way for the virus to spread, but it is not the only way. The sharing of needles and syringes by users of illegal drugs is the second most common way the AIDS virus is spread. And yes, it is possible to transmit the AIDS virus if needles are shared for tattooing or even ear-piercing. The virus also can be passed from an infected mother to her baby before or during birth. It also has been spread to persons who have received transfusions of blood from donors who were infected with the AIDS virus. However, the procedures that are now used to test blood donations have just about eliminated the risk to persons who receive blood.

The AIDS virus lives in blood, semen, and vaginal secretions. The virus may enter the body of anyone coming in contact with infected body fluids in one of the ways we have already mentioned. AIDS is not spread through casual contact. A boy or girl with AIDS who attends your school is not a threat to you. Using a toilet or a drinking fountain that has been used by someone with AIDS does not endanger you. Neither does playing sports or eating with someone who has AIDS.

Because AIDS symptoms may not appear until long after a person has been infected, it is not always possible to tell

whether or not a person has AIDS. Therefore the only way to be completely safe is the avoidance of all behavior that puts a person at risk, including the old ritual of becoming blood brothers or sisters.

Since sexual contact is the way STDs are spread and the main way HIV is spread, responsible sexual behavior is the best prevention. For single young persons, responsible sexual behavior means abstinence—waiting to become sexually active. For adults, responsible sexual behavior means a faithful commitment to one person. Persons who are sexually active are advised to reduce the risk of exposure by always using a condom properly when engaging in sexual activity. And yes, you can be tested for HIV before having sexual intercourse. This is unnecessary if you have never had intercourse, but it makes sense if one or both persons have had sexual partners in the past.

There is no way to be absolutely certain that the person you're having sex with or anticipate having sex with hasn't been exposed to HIV or another STD. That's another reason why making good decisions about sex from the very beginning is so important, and why honesty is so important to our relationships.

Persons' lives change. Some who have engaged in risky behavior eventually see their foolishness and receive forgiveness. The Bible tells the story of the woman caught committing adultery—having sexual intercourse with someone other than her husband—who was brought to Jesus. Those who brought her were ready to stone her to death for her sin. Jesus pointed out that they too were sinners and had no right to judge the woman. Jesus forgave her and said, "Go your way, and from now on do not sin again" (John 8:1-11).

A person who has been exposed to HIV may pass it on

before developing AIDS symptoms. This means that persons must be honest with husbands, wives, or other sex partners about past risky behavior. That kind of honesty is seldom easy; but considering the tragedy of AIDS, it becomes absolutely essential. One can be forgiven but cannot forget or try to hide the past.

# Pornography

Is it wrong to look at pictures of naked people?

I vaguely remember when I was about your age and one of my friends invited me to examine the stash of magazines he had found out in the woods in an older boy's hideout. Pictures of naked women! Few boys are going to pass up that opportunity!

Today no one has to head for the woods. The same kind of stuff is available right at home (or at school or in the local library) to anyone with a computer and Internet access. But we're no longer just talking about pictures of naked women or naked men. We have access to stories, photographs, and

133

videos of every possible sex act, even involving young persons, right at our fingertips.

Some folks estimate that well over half of everything available on the Internet could be classified as **pornography** (pore-NAHG-ruh-fee). Pornography is much more than pictures of naked people. Remember that those naked people were God's good creation before anyone got around to wrapping them up in a diaper and a blanket!

Under the category of pornography are materials containing images of women as objects rather than persons; condoning rape; promoting sexual relations between children and between adults and children; and linking sex with violence. Pornography is addictive, just as is alcohol, tobacco, and many other drugs. Instead of affirming the beauty of the human body and the goodness of God's gift of sexuality, pornographers (the persons who produce and sell pornographic material) take advantage of basic human curiosity and turn it into a money-making enterprise.

After prolonged exposure to pornography some persons not only begin to believe that the behaviors and attitudes they see there are acceptable, but they also begin to act them out. Police reports document the number of times that pornography is linked to acts of sexual violence. The only way to deal with an addiction is to avoid that which is addictive. That is precisely how I recommend dealing with pornography.

# Being Response-Able

**H**ave you ever become really frustrated while standing in front of your closet and trying to decide what to wear? In your mind you review where you're going, who's going to see you, and how they're going to react to what you have on. Maybe the color of your sweater or shirt is not an earth-shaking decision, but it's important to you. You put energy into making such decisions. Feeling tired after wrestling with choices is not unusual. Making decisions can be hard work—especially when you want those decisions to be responsible ones.

Responsible. Think of it like this: Response-able, or able to respond. What prepares us or makes us able to respond to situations and challenges in appropriate, faithful ways?

How do you prepare? Working at family relationships and building friendships are two very important ways. Decision-making, as we have said, is hard work. It is also lonely work when you have to struggle with your challenges all alone. What makes you better able to respond—more responsible? In part it's the example and the counsel of those who love you the most—your family, your friends, and the adults who serve as your mentors.

You also prepare by working at your relationship with God. Paul's reminder to the Corinthians serves us as well: "Do you not know that you are God's temple and that God's Spirit dwells in you?" Paul continues, "For God's temple is holy, and you are that temple!" (1 Corinthians 3:16-17). You are God's temple! God couldn't be any closer. The temple is where God lives. God lives in you.

You are that temple, and you are holy. To be holy means to be wonderfully different—to be set apart for a special purpose. In one way or another, God's special purpose for you is to grow in body, in wisdom, and in your ability to love God and others.

These are not easy days for you. Everything is moving too slowly or too quickly. But there is strength in learning to wait for God's timing and to watch for God's purpose to be unfolded. You were created by God—male or female. You were created to create. Many decisions await you. With God's help, and with the help of your family and friends, you will be responsible—able to respond!

Those who wait for the LORD
shall renew their strength,
they shall mount up with wings like eagles,
they shall run and not be weary,
they shall walk and not faint.

Isaiah 40:31

# GLOSSARY

The numbers at the end of the definitions direct you to the pages where you will find more information about these terms.

**abdomen** (AB-doh-men). The belly. 28

**abortion** (uh-BORE-shun). The surgical removal of an embryo or fetus from a pregnant woman's uterus before the embryo or fetus is able to survive on its own. 122

**abstinence** (AB-stuh-nuhns). Making the decision not to have sexual intercourse. The only birth control method guaranteed to be 100 percent effective. 116

**acne** (ACK-nee). Pimples or blemishes that often appear on the face, chest, back, and elsewhere on the body. Can be particularly severe during adolescence and demands special care. 62

**acquired immune deficiency syndrome** (uh-KWIRED ih-MUNE duh-FISH-uhn-see SIN-drohm) or **AIDS**. A disease caused by the Human Immunodeficiency Virus (HIV). AIDS causes the breakdown of the body's immune system, making it impossible for the body to fight off other diseases. AIDS is transmitted by the exchange of body fluids—primarily through sexual intercourse but also through the sharing of needles by drug users and from infected mothers to their babies. 129

**adolescence** (a-doh-LES-sens). The period of growth between childhood and adulthood. A young person going through this period is referred to as an **adolescent** (a-doh-LES-sent). 15

**AIDS**. See acquired immune deficiency syndrome. 129

**amnion** (AM-nee-uhn) or **amniotic** (am-nee-AH-tik) **sac**. The thin membrane sac filled with a watery fluid called amniotic fluid that surrounds and protects the developing fetus in the uterus. 88

**ampulla** (am-POOL-uh). The widened or flared-out portion of the vas deferens near the prostate gland. 36

**anus** (AY-nuhs). The opening where solid waste leaves the body. 30

**areola** (air-ee-OH-lah). The darker area of the breast that surrounds the nipple. 44

**birth control**. Preventing conception from taking place. 120

**birth control pill**. A medication taken exactly according to the doctor's directions that prevents ovulation and therefore prevents pregnancy. 120

**bisexual** (bie-SEKS-yoo-uhl) or **bisexuality**. Being sexually active with or sexually attracted to persons of both sexes. 118

**breasts**. Two glands on the upper chest of both males and females, the growth of which is stimulated at puberty. In females, the breasts develop so that they can produce milk when the female gives birth to a baby. 44

**Breast Self-Examination (BSE)**. A monthly self-exam that all maturing girls and all women need to perform on their breasts, checking for changes or abnormalities. 46

**breech**. When a baby is in something other than a head-first position prior to birth. This position can complicate the delivery, sometimes making a caesarian section necessary. 93

**caesarian** (sih-ZARE-ee-uhn) **section**. Delivery of a baby by surgical incision through the abdomen. 92

**cervix** (SER-viks). The lower, narrow portion of the uterus that extends into the vagina. The cervix must open or widen in order to allow the baby to move into the vagina during birth. 34

**child molesting** (muh-LEST-ing). The sexual abuse of a child. 127

**chlamydia** (KLUH-mid-ee-uh). A sexually transmitted disease. 129

**chromosomes** (KROH-muh-sohmz). Tiny rods in the nuclei of sperm and ova that carry the inherited factors from parents. The X and Y chromosomes determine the sex of the embryo. 42

**cilia** (SILL-ee-uh). Tiny hairs such as those lining the fallopian tubes. These cilia propel the ovum through the tubes. 48

**circumcision** (sir-cum-SIZH-un). The surgical removal of the foreskin—the loose layer of skin that extends over the glans or head of the penis. One who receives this operation has been **circumcised** (SIR-cum-sized). 31

**clitoral** (KLIT-uh-rul) **hood**. Fold of skin that covers the clitoris and must be pulled back in order to see the tip of the clitoris. 28

**clitoris** (KLIT-uh-ris). The small, cylinder-shaped highly sensitive female organ located at the top of the inner labia. 28

**conception** (kuhn-SEP-shun). The fertilization of the female ovum by the male sperm, which marks the beginning of pregnancy. 80

**condom** (KON-duhm). A thin sheath, usually of rubber or latex, that looks like a long, rolled-up, oversized balloon. It is placed on the erect penis before sexual intercourse to prevent the spread of disease and/or to prevent pregnancy. 121

**conjoined twins**. Twins formed by the incomplete division of the fertilized ovum where one or more parts of the body are shared by both babies. Also called Siamese twins. 94

**contract** (kuhn-TRACT). See contractions. 90

**contractions** (kuhn-TRACK-shuns). The sudden shortening of the muscles in the uterus that push the baby into the vagina and out of the mother's body. 90

**date rape**. When a female is forced against her will to have sex with someone she is dating. 127

**delivery**. The baby leaving the mother's body. 90

**diaphragm** (DIE-uh-fram). A soft rubber dome or cap that is filled with a spermicide and inserted into the vagina before sexual intercourse to prevent pregnancy. 121

**dilate** (DIE-late). The opening or widening of the cervix, allowing for the vaginal delivery of a baby. 90

**ejaculation** (e-JACK-yoo-LAY-shun). The release or squirting of semen from the penis caused by the squeezing of muscles and the prostate gland during orgasm. 36

**embryo** (EM-bree-oh). An unborn human from about the eighth day after conception until the third month of pregnancy. 88

**endometrium** (ehn-doh-MEE-tree-uhm). The lining of the uterus. 34

**139**

**epididymis** (ep-uh-DID-uh-mis). A mass of tiny tubes attached to the back of each testicle; the sperm cells mature as they move through the tubes. 36

**erect** (ih-REKT) or **erection** (ih-RECK-shun). The enlargement and hardening of the penis or the clitoris as sexual stimulation causes blood to rush to the genital area, filling tiny hollow sacs inside the shaft. 55

**estrogen** (ESS-truh-juhn). The female sex hormone that is produced primarily in the ovaries and is responsible for menstruation and for the development of secondary sex characteristics such as breast development and widened hips. 43

**fallopian** (fuh-LOH-pee-unh) **tubes**. The two tubes that branch out from either side of the upper part of the uterus, through which the ova pass from the ovaries to the uterus. 34

**feminine** (FEHM-uh-nin). Qualities associated with being female. **Femininity** (fehm-uh-NIN-uh-tee) is how a person expresses her understanding of what it means to be female. 76

**fertilization** (FER-tuhl-uh-ZAY-shun). The union of sperm cell nucleus with the nucleus of the ovum to start a new baby. Also called conception. 86

**fetus** (fee-TUHS). An unborn human from about the third month of pregnancy until birth. 88

**follicle** (FALL-uh-kuhl). Tiny sacs in the ovaries that each contain an ovum. 47

**foreplay** (FOR-play). Sex play that precedes and prepares persons for sexual intercourse. Also called pleasuring. 84

**foreskin** (FOR-skin). The loose layer of skin that covers the glans or head of a male's penis at birth. 31

**fraternal**. A multiple birth that began with the release of more than one ovum and the fertilization of those ova by different sperm. 94

**gay**. A homosexual person; more specifically, a male homosexual. 118

**gender**. Being male or female. 42

**genes** (jeenz). The part of every body cell, located on the chromosomes, that carries information about characteristics that one inherits from either or both parents. 42

**genital herpes** (HER-peez). A sexually transmitted disease. 129

**genital warts**. A sexually transmitted disease. 129

**genitals** (JEN-uh-tuhls) or **genitalia** (JEN-uh-TAIL-yuh). The external male and female sex organs—the penis, scrotum, and testicles in males, and the vulva in females. 28

**glans** (glanz). The head or tip of the penis or the clitoris. 28

**gonorrhea** (gahn-uh-REE-uh). A sexually transmitted disease. 129

**hepatitis** (HEP-uh-TIE-tihs) **B**. A sexually transmitted disease. 129

**heredity** (huh-REHD-uh-tee). Characteristics passed from parents to offspring. 42

**heterosexual** (HEHT-uh-roh-SEHK-shoo-uhl) or **heterosexuality** (HEHT-uh-roh-SEHK-shoo-AL-uh-tee). Being sexually active with or sexually attracted to persons of the other sex. 118

**HIV**. See Human Immunodeficiency Virus. 131

**homosexual** or **homosexuality**. Being sexually active with or sexually attracted to persons of one's own sex. 109

**hormones** (HOR-mohns). Chemical substances, produced by glands, that regulate the functioning of other organs. 33

**Human Immunodeficiency** (ih-MYOO-noh-duh-FIH-shuhn-see) **Virus** or **HIV**. A virus that attacks the body's immune system—the system that fights off disease. Causes AIDS. Spread most frequently through sexual relations with an infected person or the sharing of needles and syringes by users of illegal drugs. 131

**hymen** (HI-muhn). A thin layer of tissue that partially covers the opening to the vagina. It may be torn during athletic activity or stretching movement, or during first sexual intercourse. Some women are born without a hymen. 30

**identical**. A multiple birth that began with the complete division of the fertilized ovum, forming two or more babies that are completely alike. 94

**implant**. Chemical birth control method preventing ovulation. Six flexible tubes are implanted under the skin in the upper arm of the woman. 121

**incest** (IN-sest). Sexual intercourse between close relatives; a practice forbidden in most cultures. 127

**injection**. Chemical birth control method preventing ovulation with an injection once every three months. 121

**intercourse**. See sexual intercourse. 83

**intimacy** (IN-tuh-muh-see). The process of building close relationships between people through getting to know and learning to accept one another. 67

**intrauterine** (in-tra-YOO-tuhr-in) **device** or **IUD**. A soft plastic birth control device that must be inserted into and removed from the uterus by a doctor. Many questions have been raised as to the safety of this means of birth control. 120

**labia** (LAY-bee-uh). Two sets of folds of skin that are part of the vulva. The outer or major labia surround the opening to the vagina. The inner or minor labia are inside and sometimes hidden by the outer labia. The word *labia* means "lips." 28

**labor**. The stage of giving birth during which the cervix dilates or opens up, allowing the contractions of the uterine muscles to push the baby from the uterus into the vagina in preparation for delivery. 90

**lesbian** (LEZ-bee-uhn). A female homosexual. 118

**lobes**. Sections inside a woman's breast where milk is produced. 44

**masculine** (MASS-kyuh-lin). Qualities associated with being male. **Masculinity** (MASS-kyuh-LINH-uh-tee) is how a person expresses his understanding of what it means to be male. 76

**masturbation** (MASS-ter-BAY-shun). The deliberate touching or stroking of one's genitals to create sexual pleasure. 47

**menopause** (MEHN-uh-pahz). The time in a woman's life—usually between the ages of 45 and 55—during which menstruation ceases and pregnancy is no longer possible. 98

**menstrual** (MEHN-stroo-uhl) **cycle**. See menstruation. 47

**menstrual period**. See menstruation. 48

**141**

**menstruation** (men-STRAY-shun). The discharge of blood, secretions, and tissue from the uterus that females experience for four to seven days, about once a month. The entire process is called the **menstrual** (MEN-struhl) **cycle**. The time during which the discharge takes place is called the **menstrual period** or simply the **period**. 47

**milk ducts** (duhkts). Tubes inside the breast through which the mother's milk flows when she is breastfeeding her baby. 44

**miscarriage** (MISS-kair-ihj). See spontaneous abortion. 94

**mons** (mahnz). A mound of flesh located just above the genital area. Beneath the mons is a pad of fat tissue that covers and protects the pubic bone. 30

**morning sickness**. The upset stomach that some pregnant women experience, particularly during the first three months of pregnancy. It is so named because it often takes place in the morning. 95

**Natural Family Planning** (NFP). A form of birth control. Requires a couple to watch for signs of ovulation—such as the woman's body temperature—and avoid sexual intercourse on days when conception is possible. 120

**nipple**. The tip of the breast. 44

**nocturnal emission** (nock-TER-nul ee-MISH-uhn). The ejaculation of built-up semen that occurs during sleep and is often associated with sexual dreams. Also called a seminal emission or wet dream. 60

**orgasm** (OR-gaz-uhm). The intense and pleasant pulsing of muscles in the genital area that signals the highest point of excitement in sexual activity. 47

**ova** (OH-vah). The plural of ovum. 34

**ovaries** (OH-vuh-reez). Two almond-sized female reproductive glands in which ova develop and sex hormones are produced. 34

**ovulation** (ah-vyuh-LAY-shun). The ripening and release of an ovum from an ovary, occurring about once a month. 48

**ovum** (OH-vuhm). The female reproductive cell. 47

**penis** (PEE-nuhs). The cylinder-shaped part of the male genitals through which urine and semen pass. 31

**period**. See menstruation. 49

**pituitary** (pih-TOO-uh-tare-ee) **gland**. An endocrine gland at the base of the brain. Secretes a number of hormones to control body processes. 43

**placenta** (pluh-SEN-tuh). A spongy organ containing a network of blood vessels that develops on the lining of the uterus during pregnancy; it enables the exchange of food, oxygen, and waste materials between mother and child. 88

**pleasuring**. Sex play, sometimes preceding and preparing persons for sexual intercourse. See foreplay. 84

**pornography** (pore-NAHG-ruh-fee). Materials containing images of women as objects rather than as persons; condoning rape; promoting sexual relations between children and between adults and children; and linking sex with violence. 134

**pregnancy** (PREG-nun-see). The period from conception to birth. The condition of having a developing embryo or fetus within the female body. 34

**142**

**prenatal** (pree-NAY-tuhl) **care**. Medical care for mothers and babies during pregnancy. 116

**prostate** (PROSS-tate) **gland**. An organ surrounding the male urethra that secretes part of the seminal fluid. The squeezing action of the prostate helps force the semen out through the urethra during ejaculation. 36

**prostitute** (PROSS-tuh-toot). A person who is paid to perform sexual acts. 124

**puberty** (PEW-bur-tee). The period when the body changes from that of a child to that of an adult; the sex organs mature and begin to produce mature ova or sperm. 42

**pubic** (PEW-bick) **hair**. Coarse, curly hair that grows in the genital area. 44

**rape**. Forced sexual intercourse. 127

**rapist** (RAY-pist). Someone who commits rape. 127

**rectum** (RECK-tum). The lower end of the large intestine, ending at the anus. 35

**sanitary napkin**. A pad of absorbent cotton worn inside the underpants to absorb the menstrual discharge. 49

**scrotum** (SKRO-tum). The pouch of skin beneath the penis that contains the testicles. 33

**semen** (SEE-muhn). The whitish fluid ejaculated from the penis during orgasm. Also called seminal fluid. 36

**seminal vesicles** (SEM-uh-nuhl VESS-ih-kuhls). Two small pouches located at the back of the male prostate gland, where semen is produced. 36

**sexual abuse**. When one person uses sexual actions or sexual language to hurt, frighten, embarrass, or take advantage of another person. 126

**sexual intercourse**. Sexual activity where the penis is inserted into the vagina. 83

**sexuality**. The sum of a person's sexual orientation, characteristics, and behaviors.

**sexually transmitted diseases (STDs)**. A variety of diseases that are passed from one person to another through sexual activity. 125

**sexual orientation** (or-ee-en-TAY-shun). Whether one is sexually attracted to or sexually active with one's own sex, the other sex, or persons of both sexes. 118

**shaft**. The cylinder-shaped portion of the penis or of the clitoris. 28

**syphilis** (SIF-uh-luhs). A sexually transmitted disease. 129

**sperm**. Male reproductive cells produced in the testicles. 33

**spermicide** (SPER-mih-side). A sperm-killing chemical foam, cream, or jelly inserted deep in the vagina prior to sexual intercourse. 121

**spontaneous abortion** (spah-TAY-nee-uhs ah-BORE-shuhn). When the mother's body expels an embryo or fetus from the uterus before it is mature enough to survive, usually due to some abnormal development. Sometimes called a miscarriage. 94

**stereotype** (STAIR-ee-uh-type). An image that suggests what all persons within a group are or ought to be like. Stereotypes do not recognize the individuality of each person. 68

**sterilization**. The surgical process of making a person permanently incapable of reproduction. 121

143

**tampon** (TAM-pahn). A roll of absorbent material that is inserted into the vagina to absorb the menstrual discharge. 49

**testes** (TESS-tees). See testicles. 33

**testicles** (TESS-tih-kuhls). The egg-shaped male reproductive glands, suspended in the scrotum, that produce sperm and the hormone testosterone. Also known as testes. 33

**testicular** (tess-TIC-yuh-luhr) **self-examination** or **TSE**. A monthly self-exam that all maturing boys and all men need to do to check for changes or abnormalities in the testicles. 54

**testosterone** (tess-TOSS-tuh-rone). The male sex hormone, produced primarily in the testicles, which is responsible for sperm production, the full development of the genitals, and sex characteristics such as hair growth and muscle development. 54

**tubal ligation** (TOO-buhl lie-GAY-shun). A surgical procedure for sterilization in females. The fallopian tubes are cut, tied, sealed, or otherwise blocked off, either through an incision in the abdomen or through the vagina. 121

**umbilical** (umh-BILL-uh-kuhl) **cord**. The cord connecting the unborn infant to the placenta through which the fetus receives nourishment and gets rid of waste materials. 88

**urethra** (yoo-REE-thruh). The narrow tube through which urine passes out of the body from the bladder. In females the urethra is totally separate from the vagina. In males the urethra is also a part of the reproductive system, serving as a passageway for semen. 28

**uterus** (YOO-ter-us). The muscular, hollow organ in females, shaped like a light bulb or upside-down pear, in which babies grow and are nourished before birth. Also called the womb. 34

**vagina** (vuh-JIE-nuh). An elastic, muscular passage leading from the uterus to the outside of the body. Receives the erect penis during sexual intercourse and allows a baby to pass from the womb and out of the mother's body during delivery. Also referred to as the birth canal. 28

**vaginal** (VAJ-uh-nuhl) **area**. The vagina and the area of the vulva immediately around it. 47

**vas deferens** (VAZ DEHF-uhr-unhz). The tube in the male through which sperm passes from the epididymis to the seminal vesicles and urethra. Also called the spermatic duct, sperm duct, or simply the vas. 36

**vasectomy** (vah-SEHK-tuh-me). The surgical procedure for sterilization in males. On both sides of the scrotum, a small incision is made, and the vas deferens is cut, tied, sealed, or otherwise blocked off. Normal ejaculation of semen continues, but the semen no longer contains sperm. Sperm continue to be produced, but they are reabsorbed by the body. 121

**virgin**. A person who has not experienced sexual intercourse. 97

**vulva** (VUL-vuh). The external sex organ of the female. Includes the labia, clitoris, and the openings to the vagina and urethra. 28

**vulnerability** (VUHL-ner-uh-BILL-uh-tee). A weakness or an obstacle one cannot overcome. Vulnerabilities mean that we must often depend on the help of others. 68

**womb** (WOOM). See uterus. 19